BEASTS
FROM BRICKS

Amazing LEGO® Designs for Animals from Around the World

EKOW NIMAKO

Brimming with creative inspiration, how-to projects, and useful information to enrich your everyday life, Quarto Knows is a favorite destination for those pursuing their interests and passions. Visit our site and dig deeper with our books into your area of interest: Quarto Creates, Quarto Cooks, Quarto Homes, Quarto Lives, Quarto Drives, Quarto Explores, Quarto Gifts, or Quarto Kids.

First Published in 2017 by Quarry Books, an imprint of The Quarto Group,
100 Cummings Center, Suite 265-D, Beverly, Massachusetts 01915-6101, USA.
T (978) 282-9590 F (978) 283-2742 www.QuartoKnows.com

Quarry Books titles are also available at discount for retail, wholesale, promotional, and bulk purchase. For details, contact the Special Sales Manager by email at specialsales@quarto.com or by mail at The Quarto Group, Attn: Special Sales Manager, 401 Second Avenue North, Suite 310, Minneapolis, MN 55401, USA.

10 9 8 7 6 5 4 3 2 1

ISBN: 978-1-63159-299-7

Digital edition published in 2017

Library of Congress Cataloging-in-Publication Data is available

Design: Sporto
Cover Image: Janick Laurent, www.janicklaurent.com
Page Layout: Sporto
Photography: Janick Laurent, www.janicklaurent.com
Illustration: Tyler Clites

Printed in China

PREFACE

In the summer of 2013, I began sculpting my first exhibition, Building Black, a body of work that not only launched me into the Canadian art community the following year, but simultaneously reignited my long lost joy of building with LEGO®. As a child, it was not unusual for me to be found amid a colorful sea of plastic parts trying to devise a realistic plan to land a job at the mythical LEGO® headquarters in Denmark—which was, to my 6 year-old mind, equivalent to Dorothy's frolicsome campaign to find the Emerald City of Oz. But life, as it appeared nearly 30 years later, had an alternate plan for me. It was my lifelong love of art that would actually bring my true building abilities to the surface and help me carve my own path using what I call the most versatile medium in the world. This book represents a significant achievement along that path.

What I love most about using LEGO® in my practice is the unique challenge of capturing the natural forms of the beings and animals I create, especially since there's virtually an infinite assortment of shapes and objects to create them with. That said, it is really when I create simple and small that my job becomes that much more complex. The sculptures in this book took me several hours each to design, some several days, and because there are so few parts to work with on such a small scale, expressing the subtleties of these beautiful beasts required a keen attention to detail, and a masterful approach to sculpture. Artists are inspired by the world to make art, so art is made for the world to be inspired.

Happy building.

Special thanks to Joy Aquilino and Quarry Books for totally liking my art.

CONTENTS

AFRICAN ELEPHANT

Loxodonta africana

There is no land animal on earth larger than the African elephant, which may be why it's so emblematic of its namesake continent. For this book I decided I would build a young elephant with its trunk to the sky in order to capture its sense of wonder and play.

- Elephants use their most identifiable trait (their long, prehensile trunk) for a variety of tasks, such as eating and even communicating; they touch each other with it by way of greeting, and can trumpet loudly when playing or giving a warning.

- Elephants don't sleep for long periods of time and are often mobile, traveling very far in search of greener grasslands to feed.

- It is currently illegal to hunt elephants for their ivory, but this cruel practice still exists, causing various African elephant populations to be at risk.

Parts Color Key

■	Dark Green
■	Light Bluish Gray
□	White

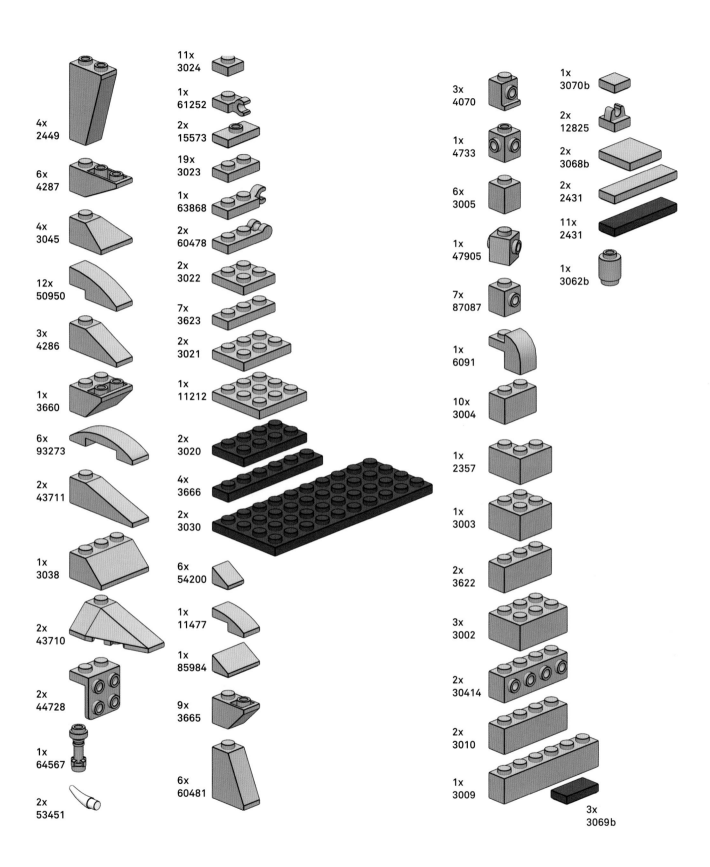

4x
2449

6x
4287

4x
3045

12x
50950

3x
4286

1x
3660

6x
93273

2x
43711

1x
3038

2x
43710

2x
44728

1x
64567

2x
53451

11x
3024

1x
61252

2x
15573

19x
3023

1x
63868

2x
60478

2x
3022

7x
3623

2x
3021

1x
11212

2x
3020

4x
3666

2x
3030

6x
54200

1x
11477

1x
85984

9x
3665

6x
60481

3x
4070

1x
4733

6x
3005

1x
47905

7x
87087

1x
6091

10x
3004

1x
2357

1x
3003

2x
3622

3x
3002

2x
30414

2x
3010

1x
3009

1x
3070b

2x
12825

2x
3068b

2x
2431

11x
2431

1x
3062b

3x
3069b

1

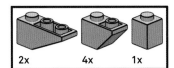

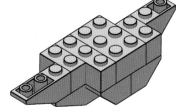

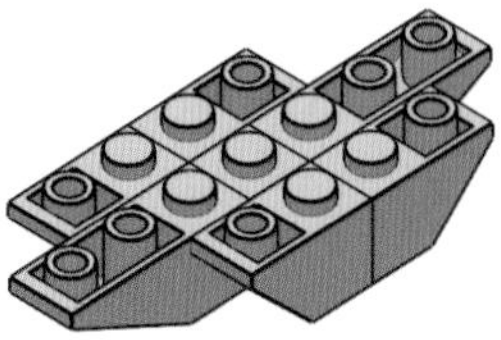

2

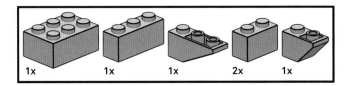

2x 1x 1x 1x 1x

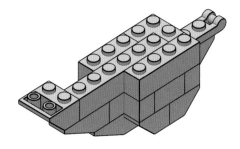

3

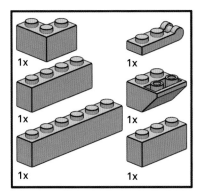

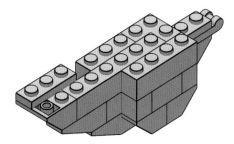

4

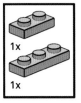

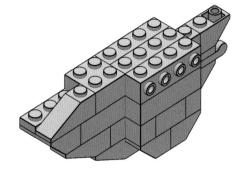

5

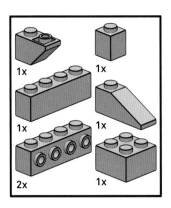

6

1x

1x

7

2x

1x

1x   1x

8

1x

1x

9

1x

1x

1x

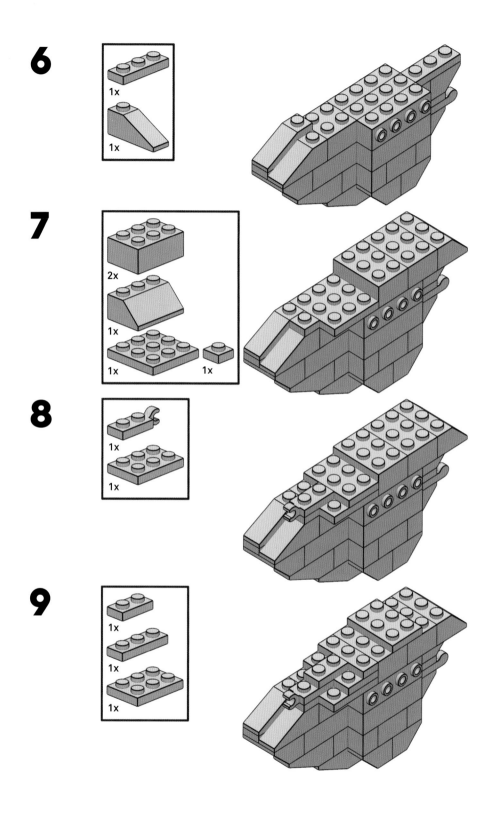

10

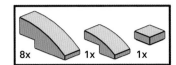

8x   1x   1x

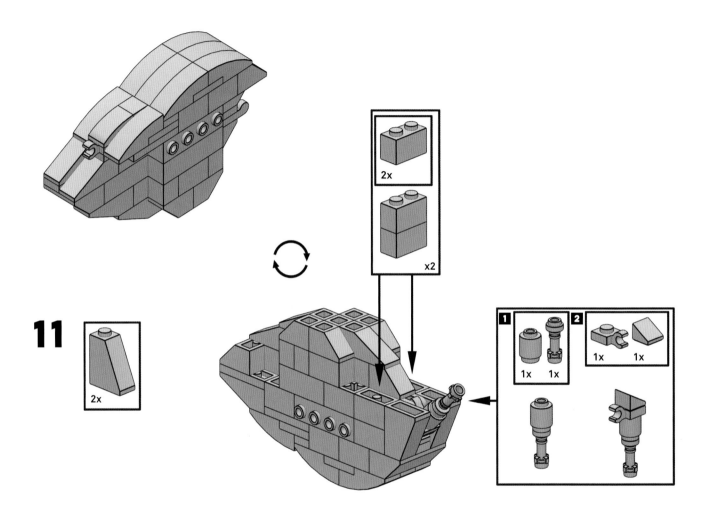

2x

x2

1	2
1x 1x	1x 1x

11

2x

1

1x   1x

1

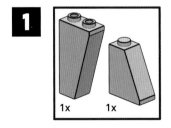

1x   1x   1x

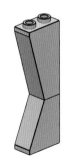

2

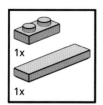
1x
1x

1 1x **2** 1x

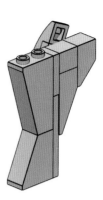
2

12

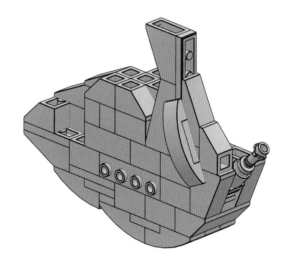

1
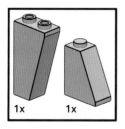
1x 1x

1 1x 1x 1x

2

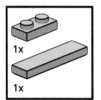

1 1x   **2** 1x

 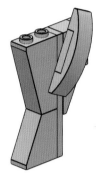

13

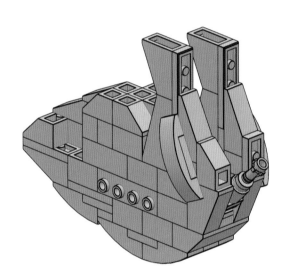

1

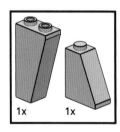 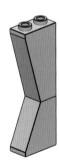

1x   1x

2

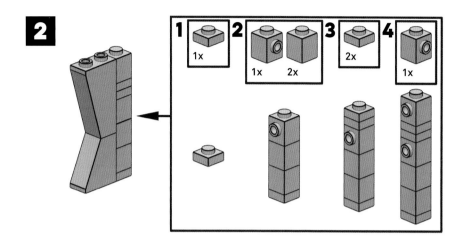

3

4

5

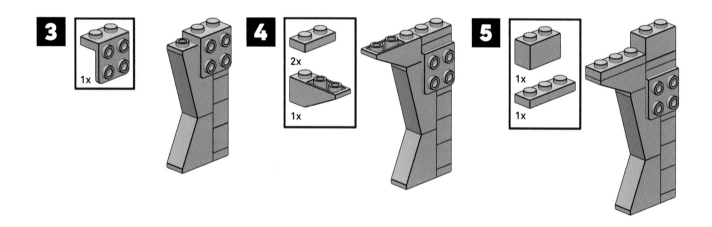

6

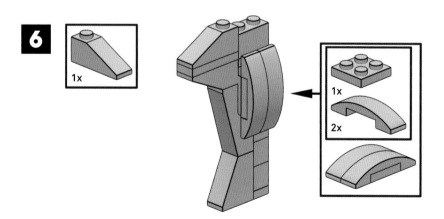

14

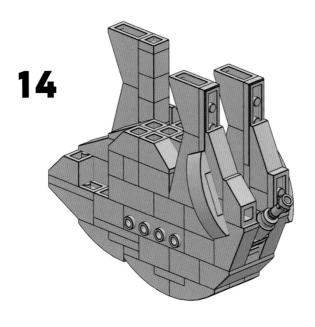

1

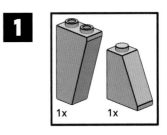

1x   1x

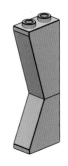

2

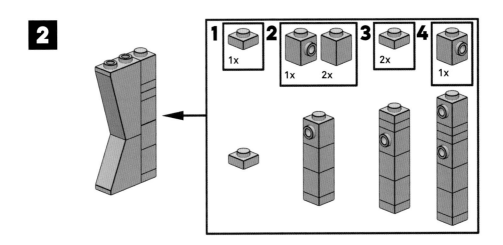

1 1x **2** 1x 2x **3** 2x **4** 1x

3

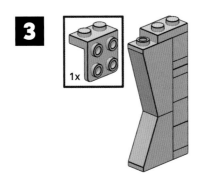

1x

4

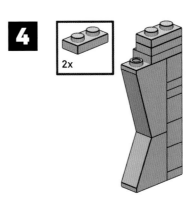

2x

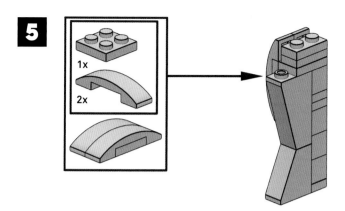

5

15

16

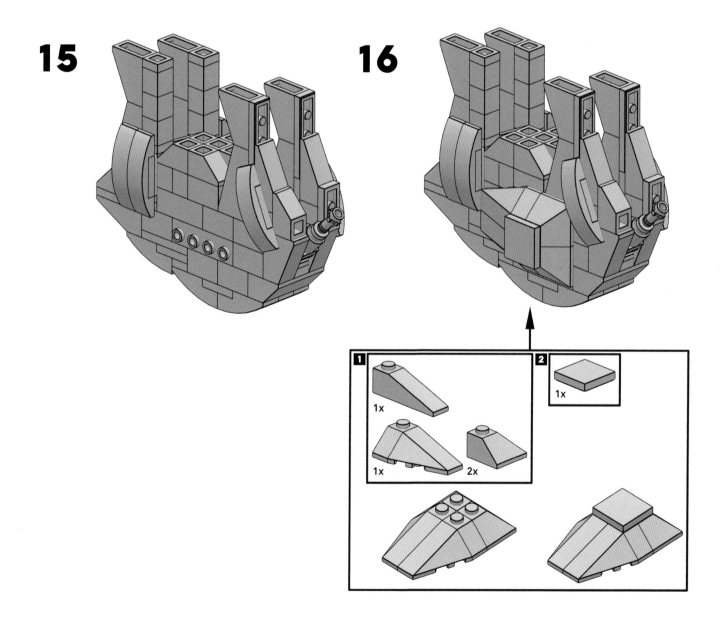

17

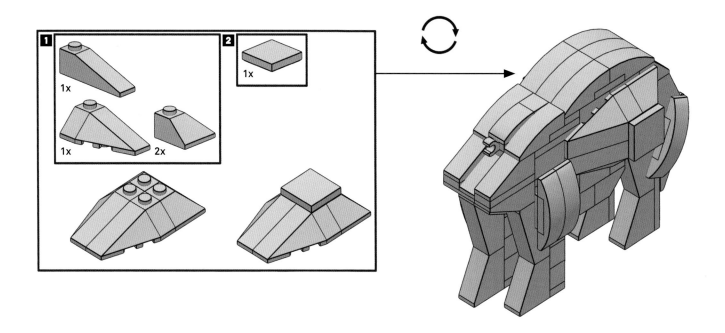

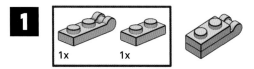

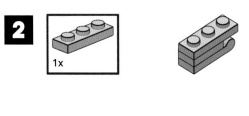

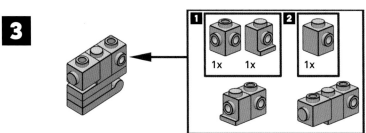

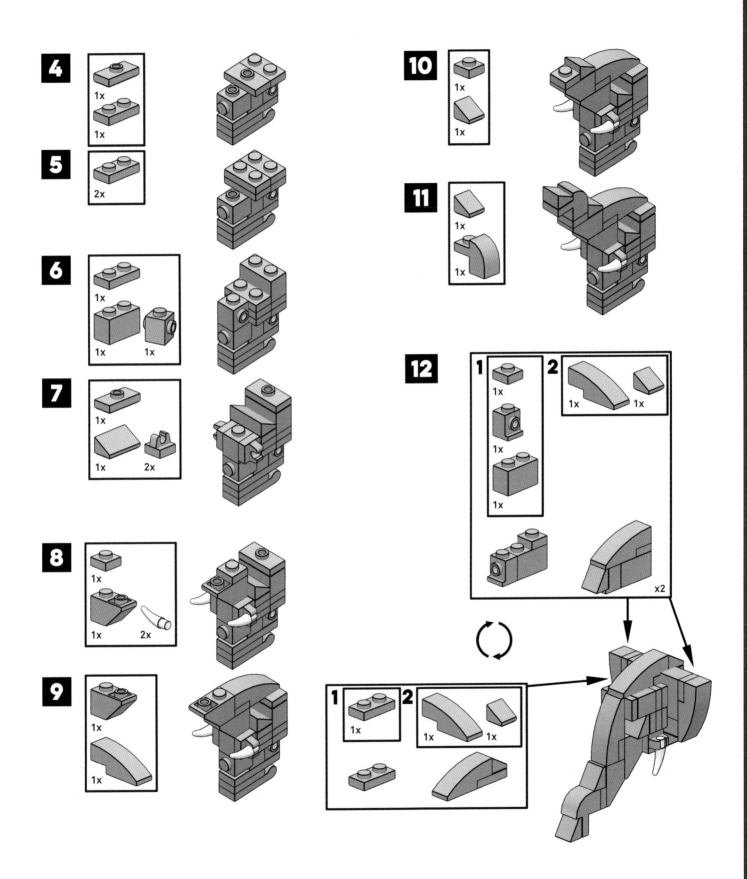

18

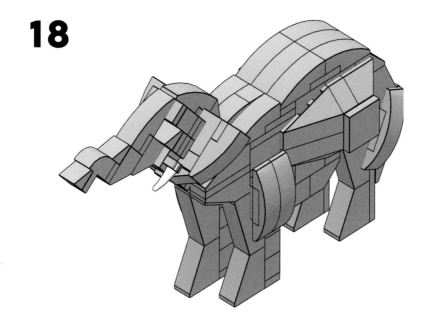

1

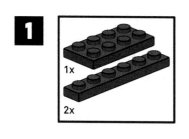

1x

2x

2

1x

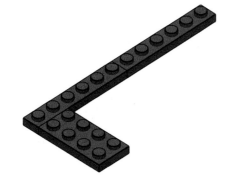

3

1x
2x

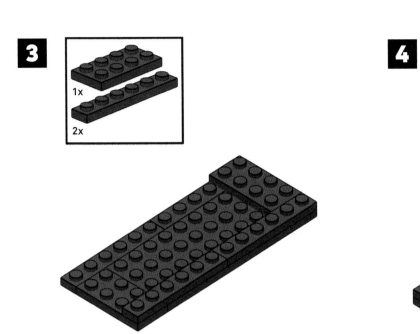

4

1x

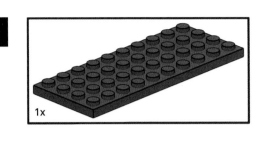

5

3x
2x
2x
11x

19

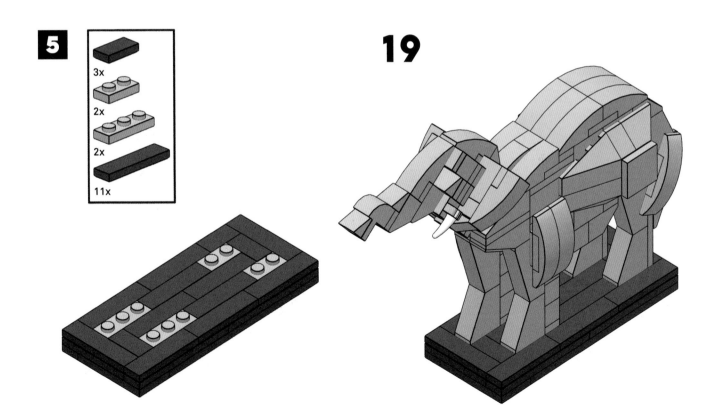

ROAN ANTELOPE

Hippotragus equinus

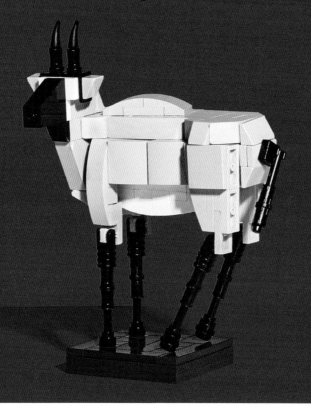

I've always admired this species of antelope and thought it would be a great choice to represent the beauty of African wildlife. I enjoyed the process of building its legs most of all since I'd never built this sort of ungulate before, and it was an immense challenge to figure out how to capture their strong but graceful limbs.

- Female roan antelopes can breed all year long, but births are much less common during the dry season.

- Male roan antelopes can have ferocious confrontations with one another when their position of dominance is at stake. Their hooves and horns become formidable weapons when it comes to a dust-up.

- Due to habitat loss and poaching, the roan antelope is currently locally extinct in two African countries and is still threatened elsewhere on the continent for the same reasons.

Parts Color Key

■	Black
■	Light bluish gray
■	Reddish brown
■	Tan
□	White

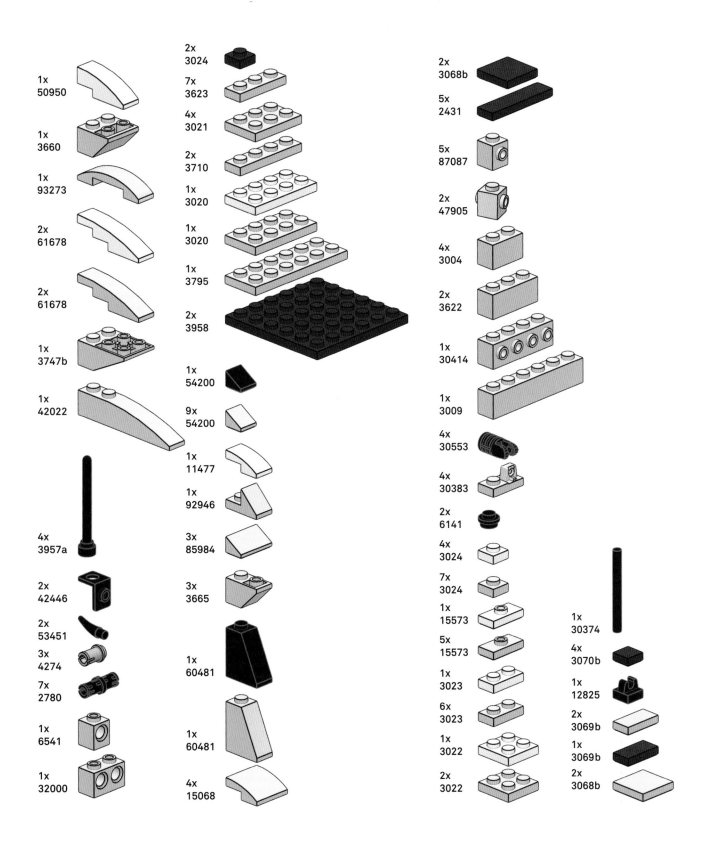

1x
50950

1x
3660

1x
93273

2x
61678

2x
61678

1x
3747b

1x
42022

4x
3957a

2x
42446

2x
53451

3x
4274

7x
2780

1x
6541

1x
32000

2x
3024

7x
3623

4x
3021

2x
3710

1x
3020

1x
3020

1x
3795

2x
3958

1x
54200

9x
54200

1x
11477

1x
92946

3x
85984

3x
3665

1x
60481

1x
60481

4x
15068

2x
3068b

5x
2431

5x
87087

2x
47905

4x
3004

2x
3622

1x
30414

1x
3009

4x
30553

4x
30383

2x
6141

4x
3024

7x
3024

1x
15573

5x
15573

1x
3023

6x
3023

1x
3022

2x
3022

1x
30374

4x
3070b

1x
12825

2x
3069b

1x
3069b

2x
3068b

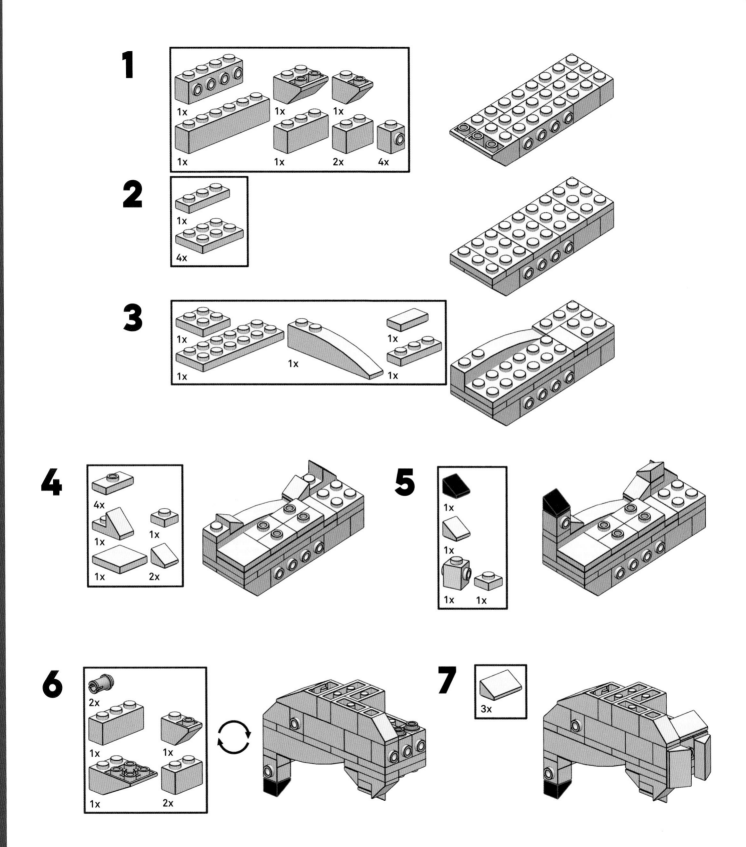

8

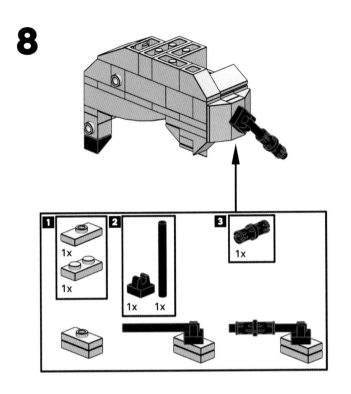

1 1x 1x

2 1x 1x

3 1x

5 1x

1 1x **2** 1x 1x

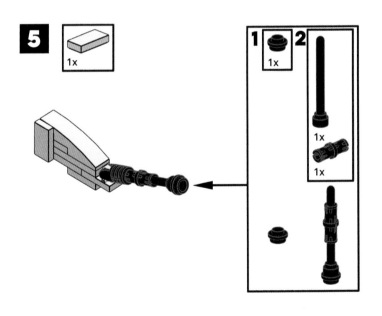

1 1x

2 1x 1x

3 1x 1x 1x

4 1x 1x

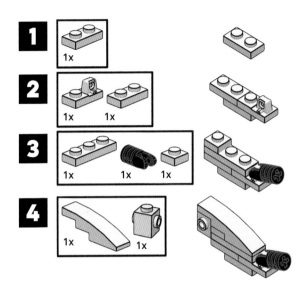

9

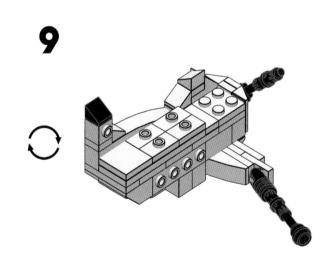

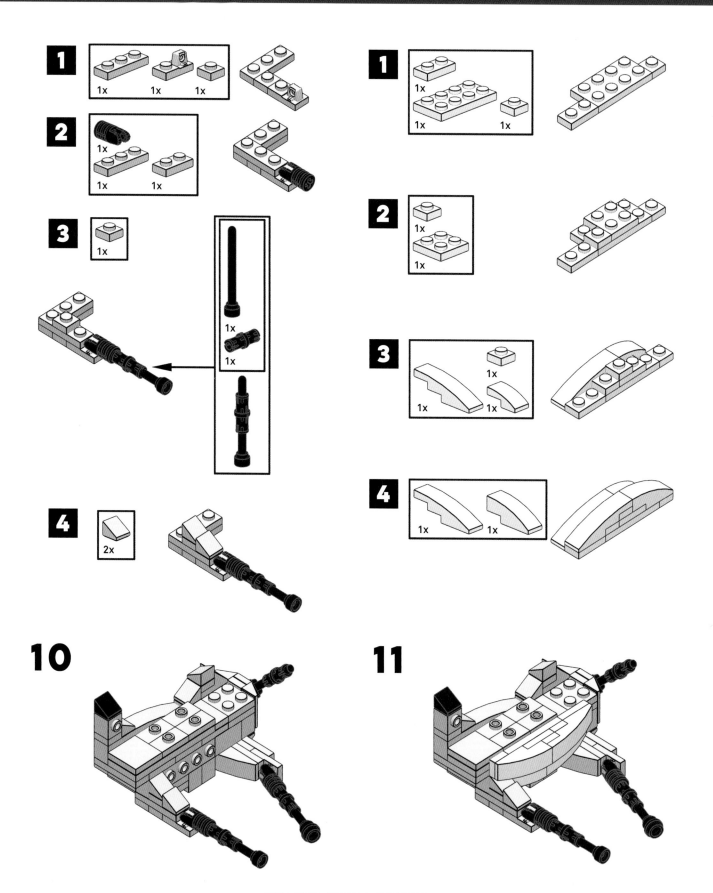

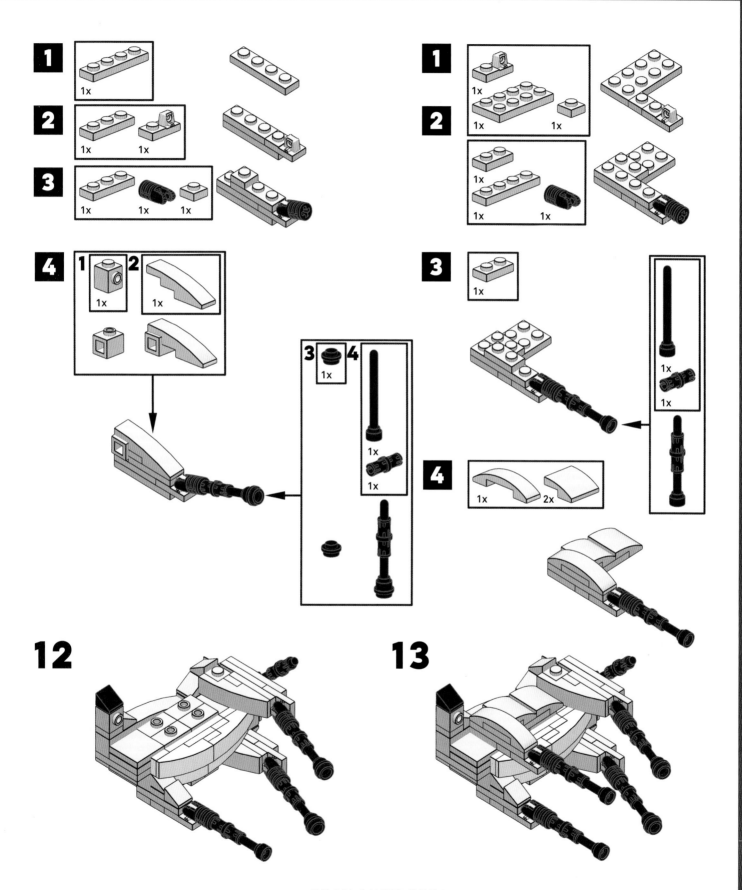

14

1x

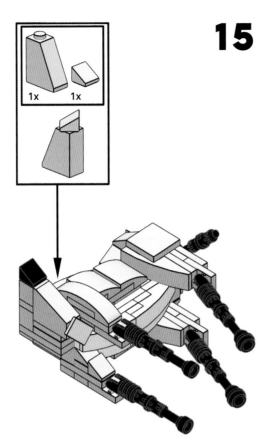

1x 1x

15

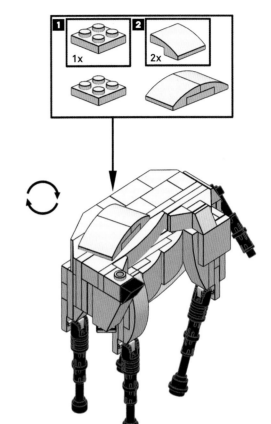

1 1x

2 2x

1
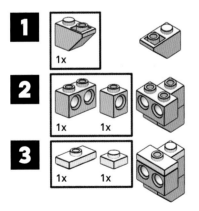
1x

2
1x

3
1x 1x

4
1x

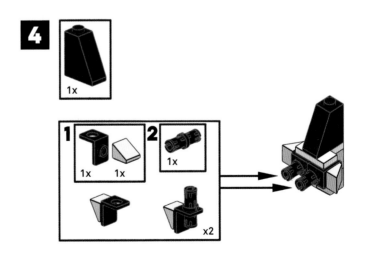

1 1x 1x

2 1x

x2

5 1x

6 2x 1x

16

1 2x

2 1x 2x 5x 4x 2x

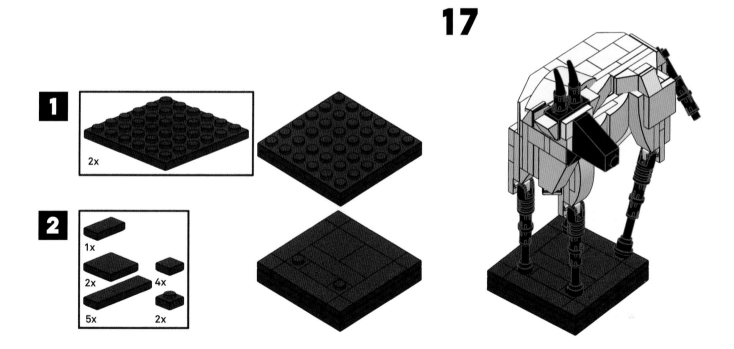

17

HIPPOPOTAMUS

Hippopotamus amphibious

Hippos can weigh up to 8,000 pounds (3,600 kg) and are surprisingly good swimmers. With their eyes, nostrils, and ears sitting high on their heads, they can easily stay submerged underwater for minutes at a time. I've always been a fan of this bulbous and somewhat amphibious beast, and thought it would be best to depict it as if it were elegantly floating just below the surface of a river.

- At one time, hippos were found across sub-Saharan Africa, but their number have since declined and they are mostly found in East Africa.

- Female hippos give birth to one calf after carrying it for approximately 8 months. Mother hippos form schools while the calves are young for safety reasons.

- Hippos secrete their own germ deterring substance, which also acts as a skin moistener that helps protect them from the intense African sun.

Parts Color Key

- Black
- Blue
- Dark Bluish Gray

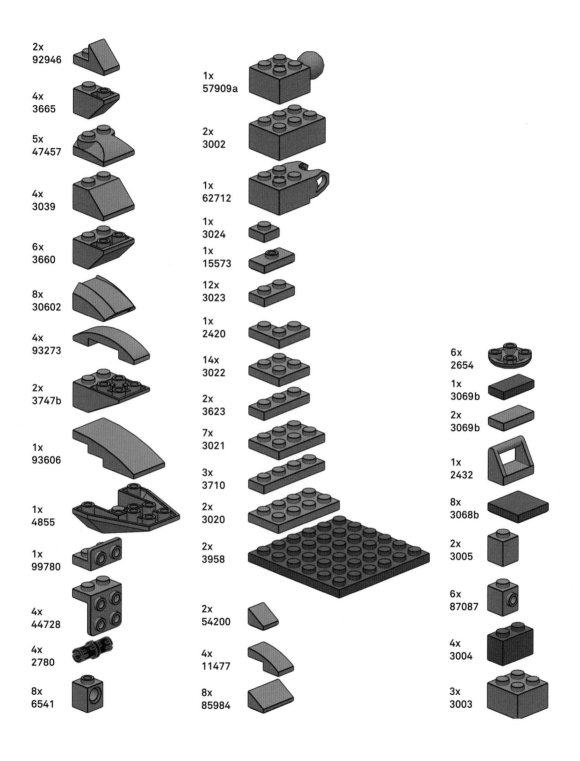

2x
92946

4x
3665

5x
47457

4x
3039

6x
3660

8x
30602

4x
93273

2x
3747b

1x
93606

1x
4855

1x
99780

4x
44728

4x
2780

8x
6541

1x
57909a

2x
3002

1x
62712

1x
3024

1x
15573

12x
3023

1x
2420

14x
3022

2x
3623

7x
3021

3x
3710

2x
3020

2x
3958

2x
54200

4x
11477

8x
85984

6x
2654

1x
3069b

2x
3069b

1x
2432

8x
3068b

2x
3005

6x
87087

4x
3004

3x
3003

1

2

3

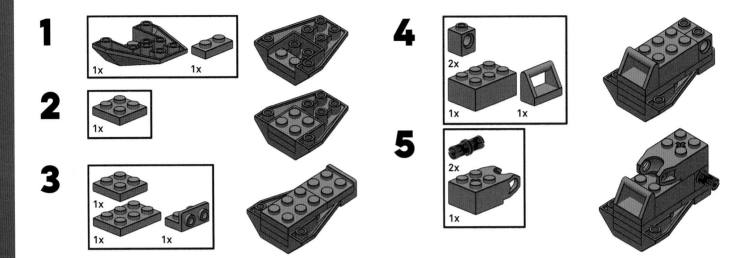

4

5

6

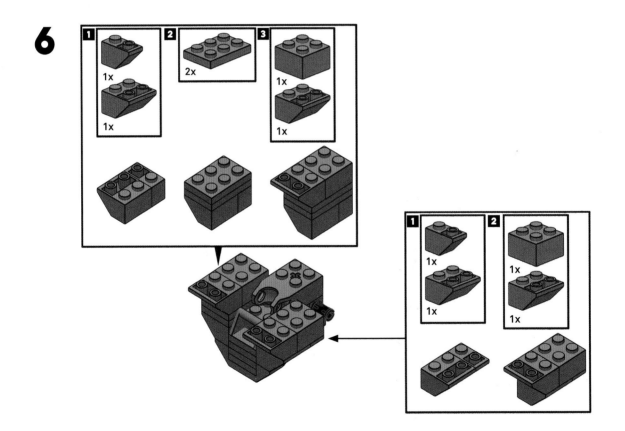

7

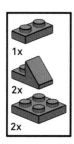

1x
2x
2x

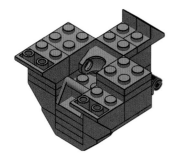

8

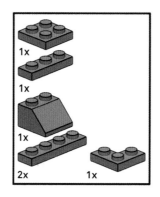

1x
1x
1x
2x   1x

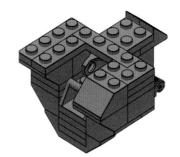

9

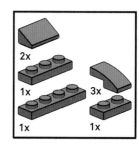

2x
1x   3x
1x   1x

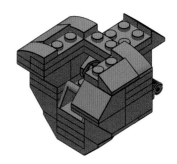

10

2x
1x

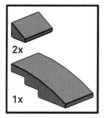

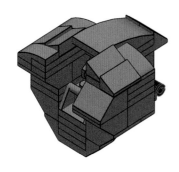

11

1 1x 1x   **2** 1x 2x   **3** 1x 1x

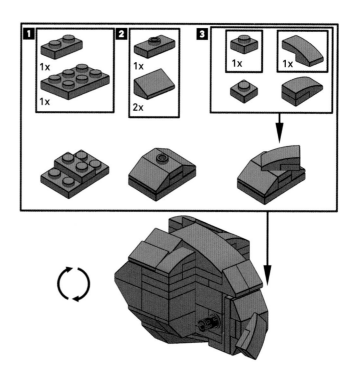

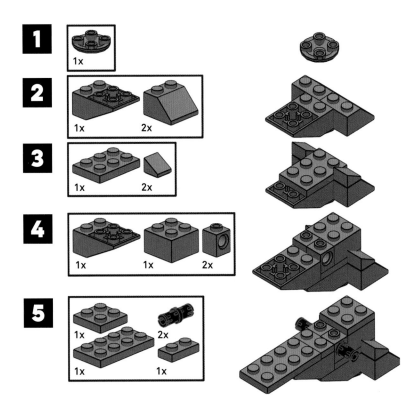

1 1x

2 1x   2x

3 1x   2x

4 1x   1x   2x

5 1x   2x   1x   1x

6 1x   1x   1x   6x

7 1x   1x

1x   1x   x2

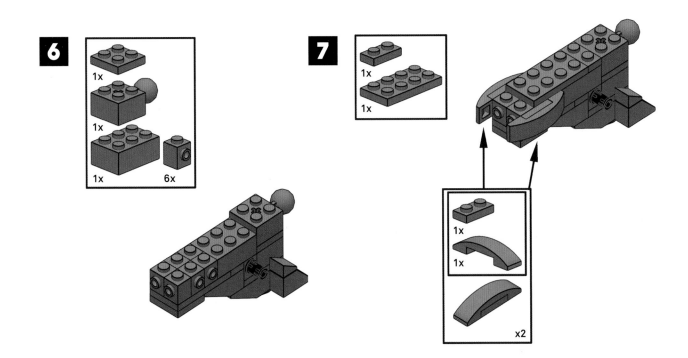

8

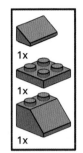
1x
1x
1x

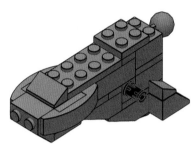

9

1x
1x
2x

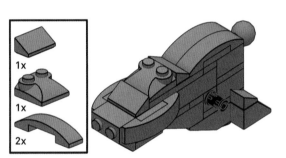

1

1x

2

1x 1x

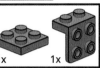

3

1x 1x 1x

4

1x
1x

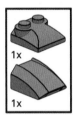

5

1x

12

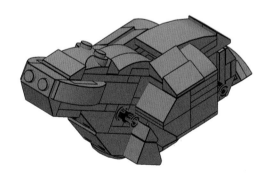

13

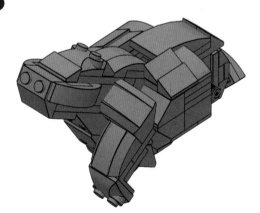

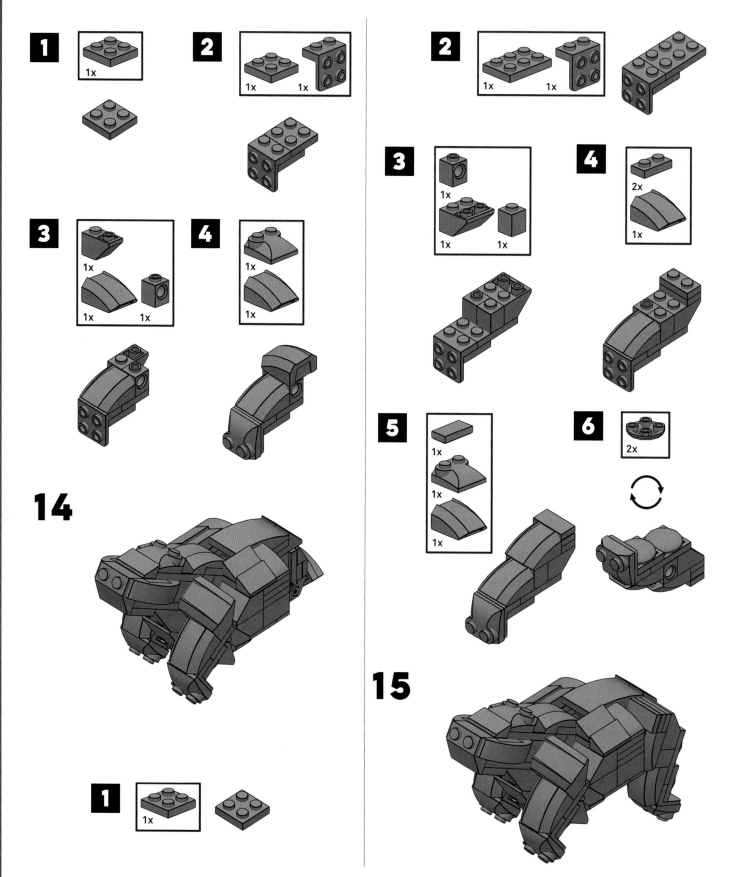

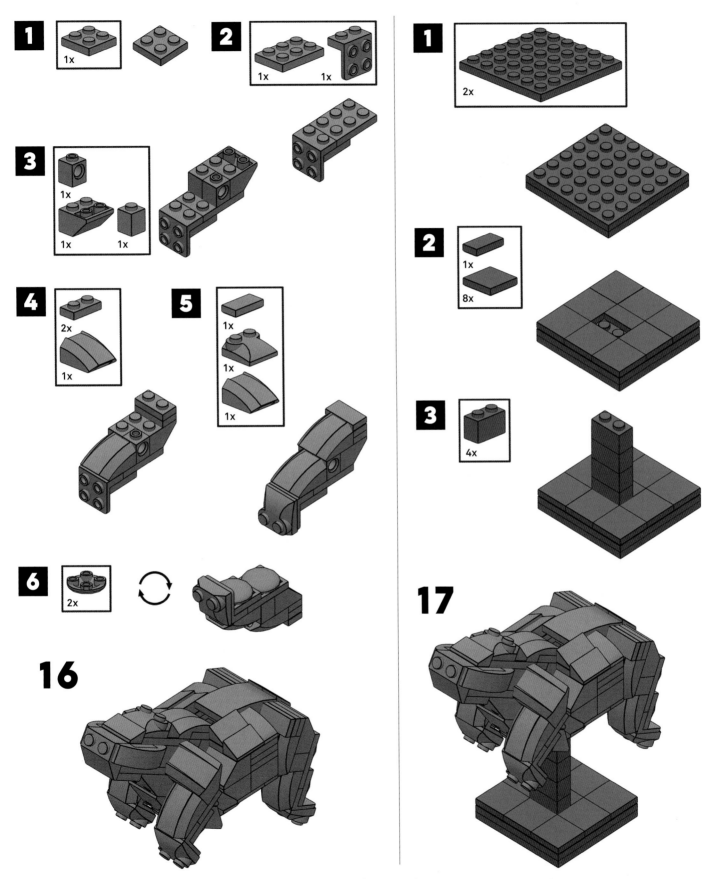

1 1x

2 1x 1x

3 1x 1x 1x

4 2x 1x

5 1x 1x 1x 1x

6 2x

16

1 2x

2 1x 8x

3 4x

17

SUFFOLK SHEEP

Ovis aries

When I consider the pastures of Ireland, Scotland, and England, only one creature comes to mind: the Suffolk sheep. With its black head and feet, fluffy white coat, and burly build, it's hard not to appreciate the significance of this wooly farm creature. Giving the sculpture a stiff posture and upraised head helped me imagine it as a haughty animal, adding a little humor to the piece.

- Suffolk sheep were originally bred in England during the 19th century.

- Suffolk sheep are solidly built and can endure virtually any kind of environment, which makes them a popular and dependable stock.

- The Suffolk sheep is not the best producer of wool and is mainly raised for food.

Parts Color Key
- ■ Black
- ■ Green
- ■ Light bluish gray
- □ White

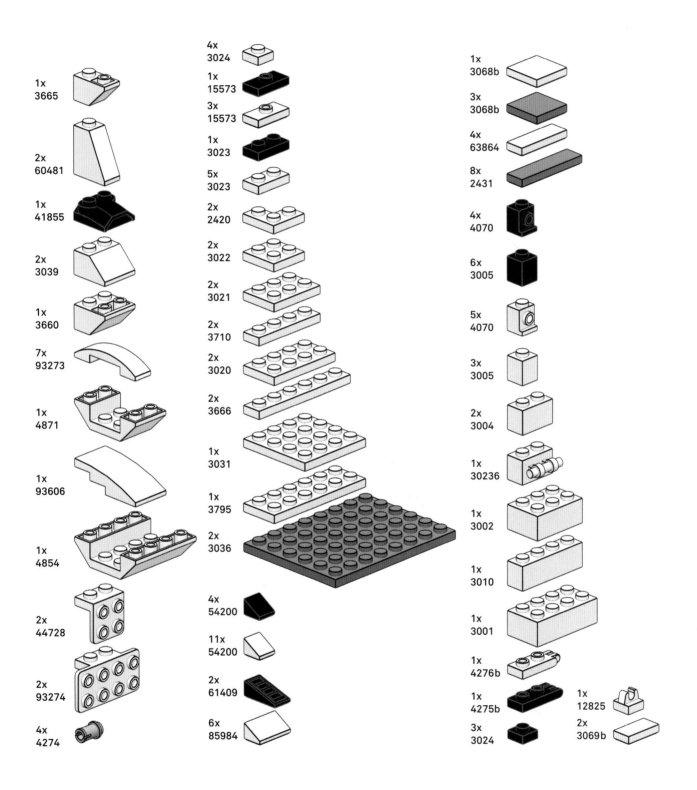

1x
3665

2x
60481

1x
41855

2x
3039

1x
3660

7x
93273

1x
4871

1x
93606

1x
4854

2x
44728

2x
93274

4x
4274

4x
3024

1x
15573

3x
15573

1x
3023

5x
3023

2x
2420

2x
3022

2x
3021

2x
3710

2x
3020

2x
3666

1x
3031

1x
3795

2x
3036

4x
54200

11x
54200

2x
61409

6x
85984

1x
3068b

3x
3068b

4x
63864

8x
2431

4x
4070

6x
3005

5x
4070

3x
3005

2x
3004

1x
30236

1x
3002

1x
3010

1x
3001

1x
4276b

1x
4275b

1x
12825

3x
3024

2x
3069b

1

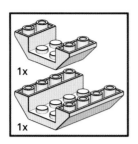

1x

1x

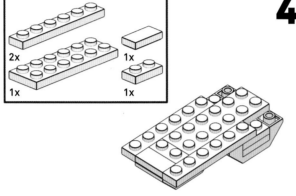

2

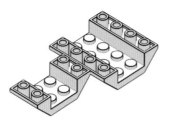

2x

2x

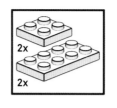

3

2x

1x

1x

1x

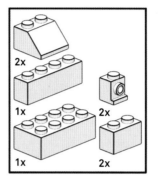

4

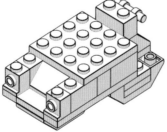

2x

1x

1x

2x

2x

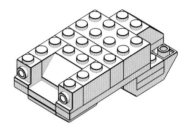

5

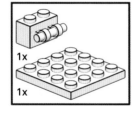

1x

1x

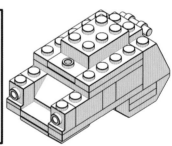

6

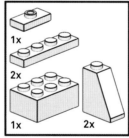

1x

2x

1x

2x

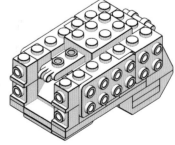

7

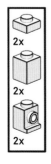

2x

2x

2x

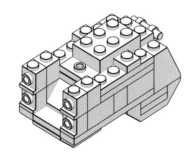

8

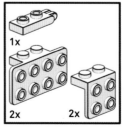

1x

2x

2x

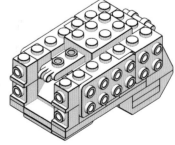

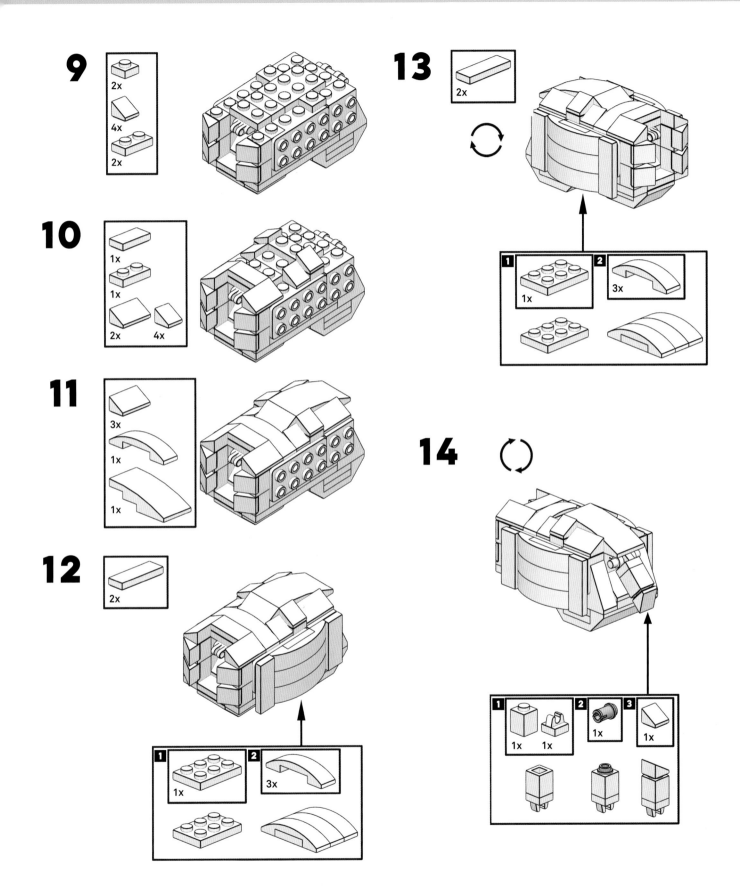

15

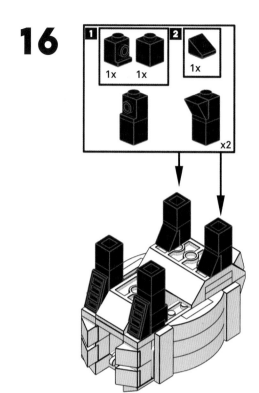

16

1
2x

2
1x

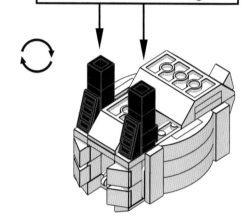

3

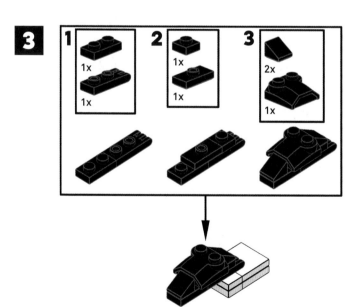

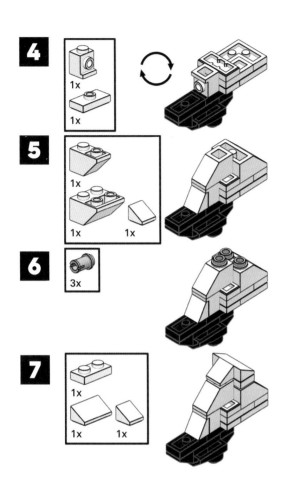

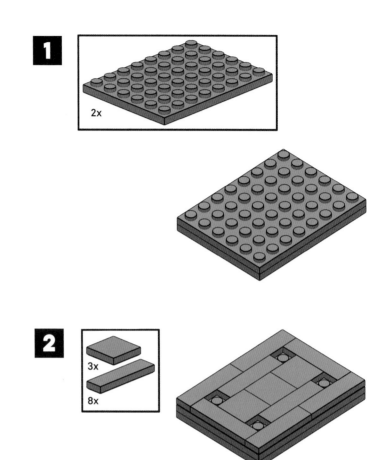

17

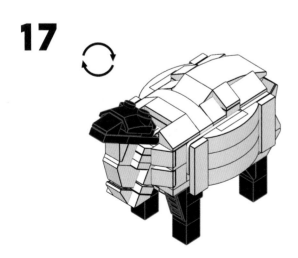

18

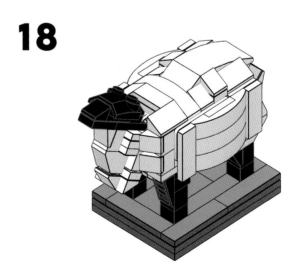

EUROPEAN BISON

Bison bonasus

With its stern, brutish demeanor, the European bison maintains a sort of avuncular charm, despite its bulky body and gruff temperament. As such, I decided to build this sculpture lying down with its head raised, as if basking in the shade after a hard day grazing in the sun.

- Unlike many other species of ungulate, both male and female European bison grow large, curved horns.

- With the exception of mating season, bison herds are segregated into male and female groups.

- European bison may seem large and cumbersome, but they are spry enough to make impressive leaps over obstacles in their path.

Parts Color Key

⬛	Black
⬛	Dark green
⬛	Light bluish gray
⬛	Reddish brown

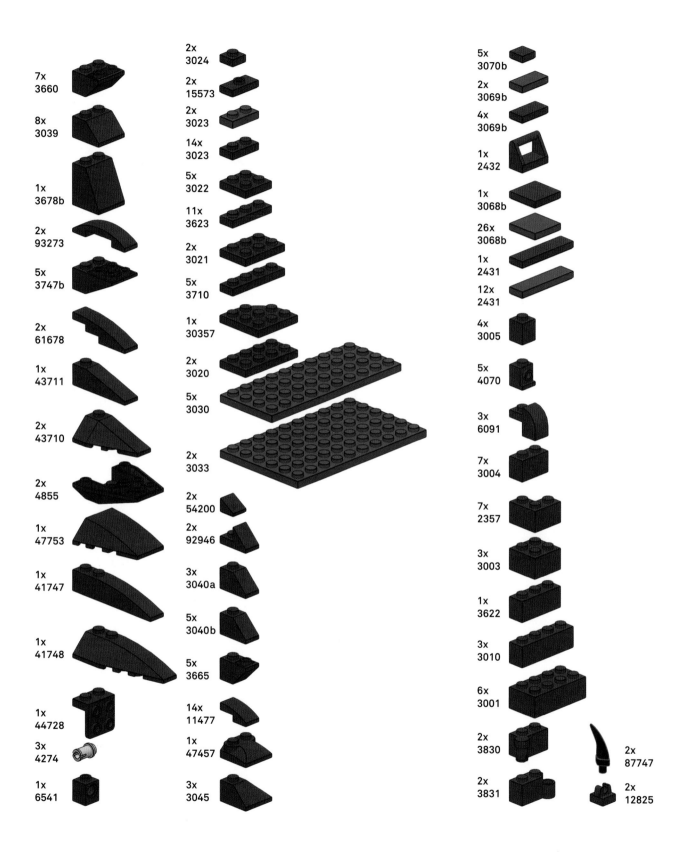

7x
3660

8x
3039

1x
3678b

2x
93273

5x
3747b

2x
61678

1x
43711

2x
43710

2x
4855

1x
47753

1x
41747

1x
41748

1x
44728

3x
4274

1x
6541

2x
3024

2x
15573

2x
3023

14x
3023

5x
3022

11x
3623

2x
3021

5x
3710

1x
30357

2x
3020

5x
3030

2x
3033

2x
54200

2x
92946

3x
3040a

5x
3040b

5x
3665

14x
11477

1x
47457

3x
3045

5x
3070b

2x
3069b

4x
3069b

1x
2432

1x
3068b

26x
3068b

1x
2431

12x
2431

4x
3005

5x
4070

3x
6091

7x
3004

7x
2357

3x
3003

1x
3622

3x
3010

6x
3001

2x
3830

2x
3831

2x
87747

2x
12825

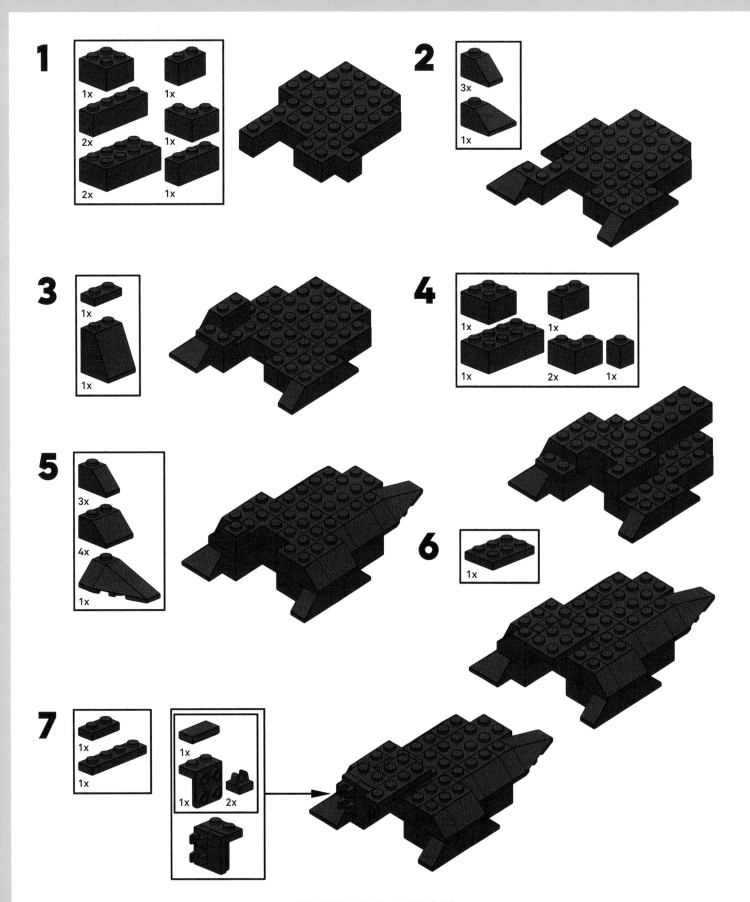

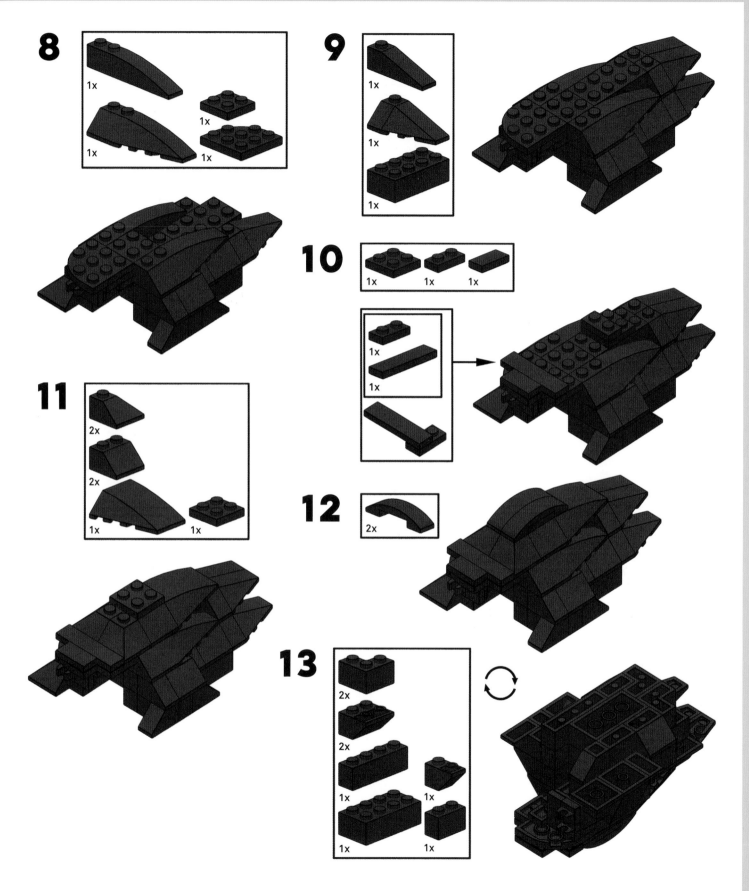

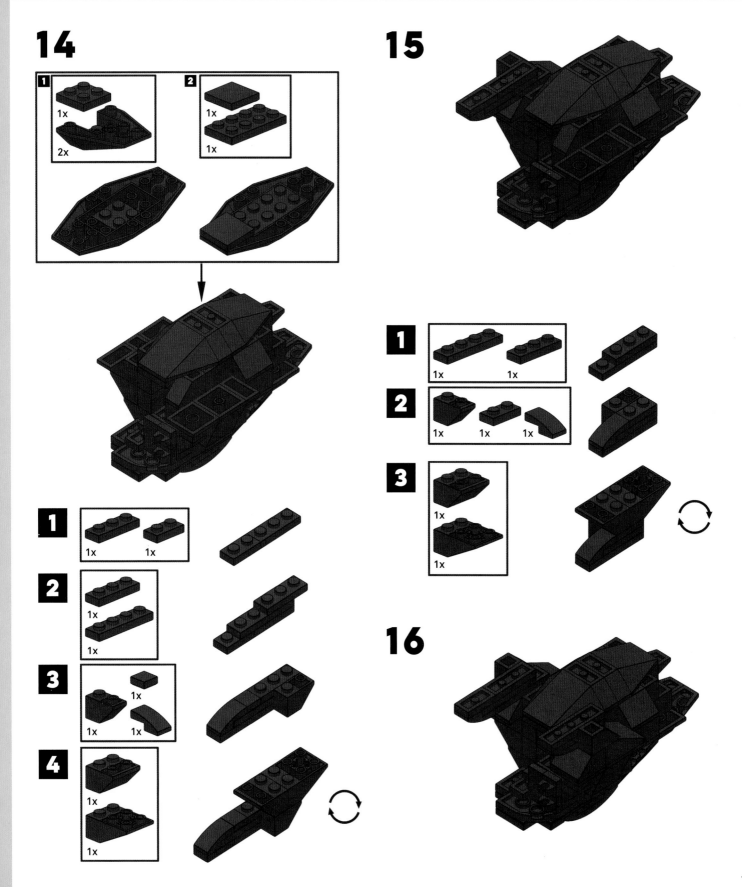

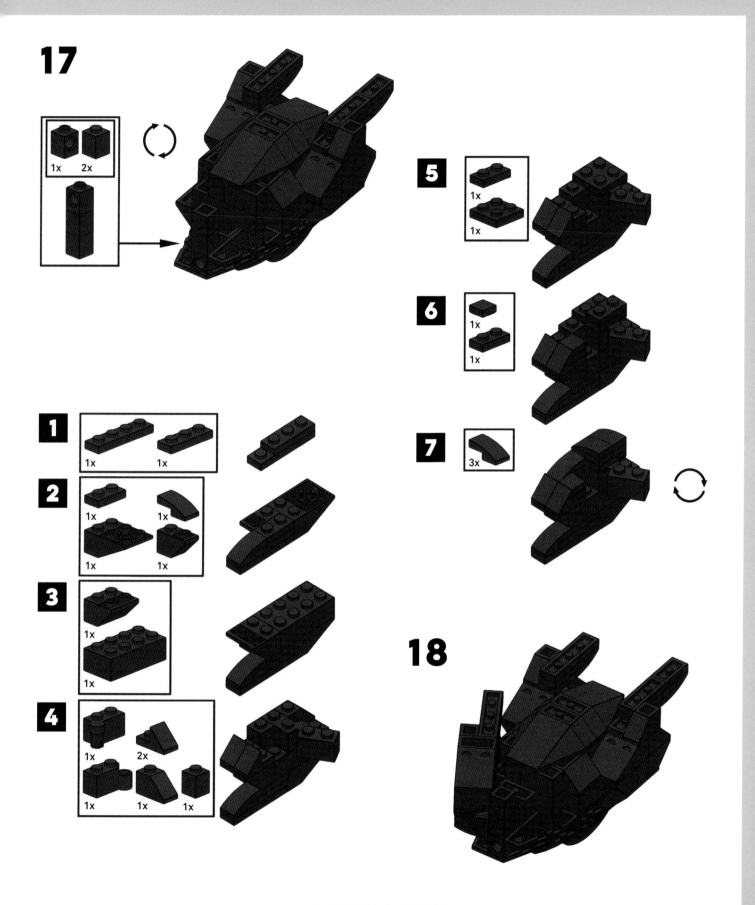

1

1x   1x

2

1x   1x
1x   1x

3

1x
1x   1x
1x   1x

4

1x
1x
1x

5

2x
1x

6

1x
1x
1x   3x

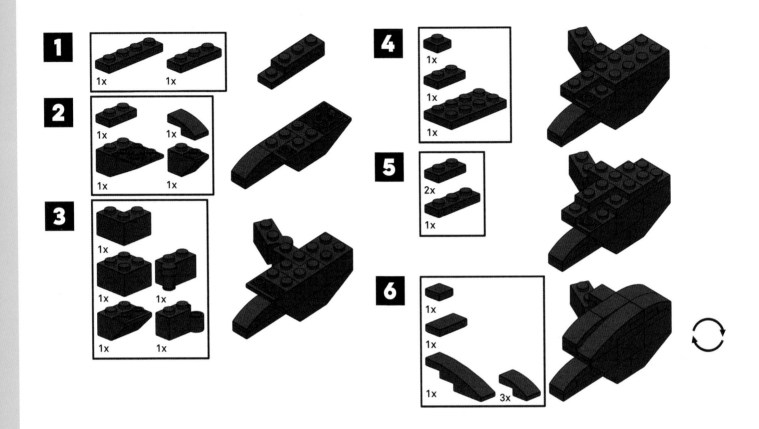

19

1x

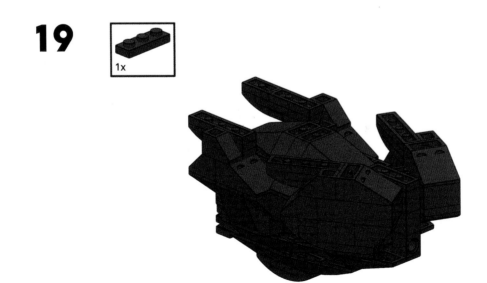

20

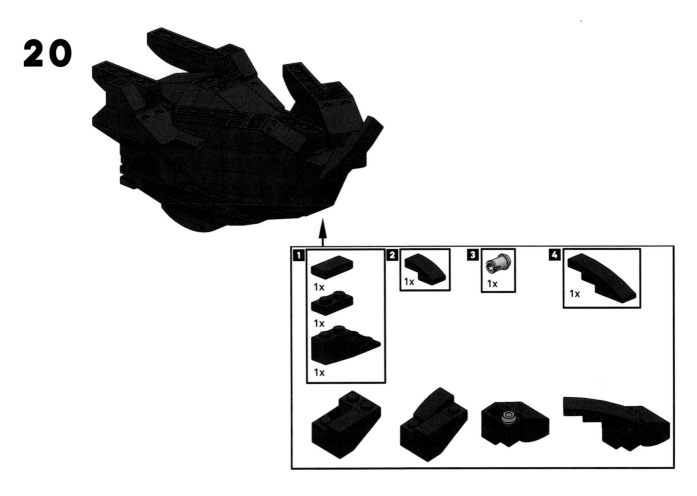

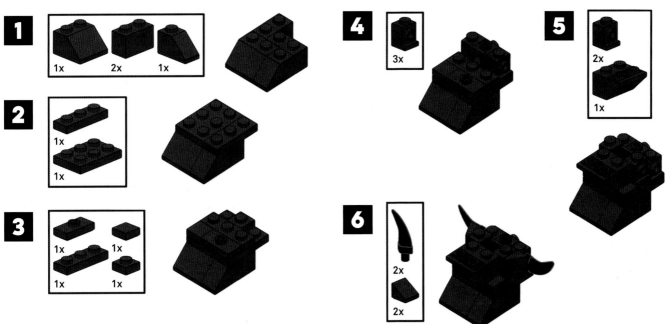

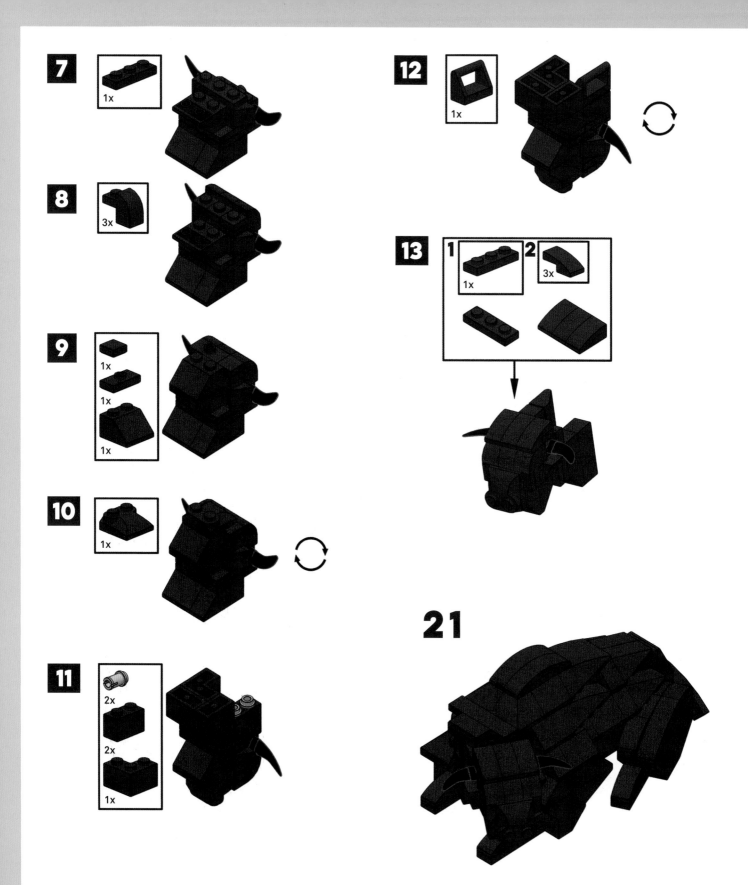

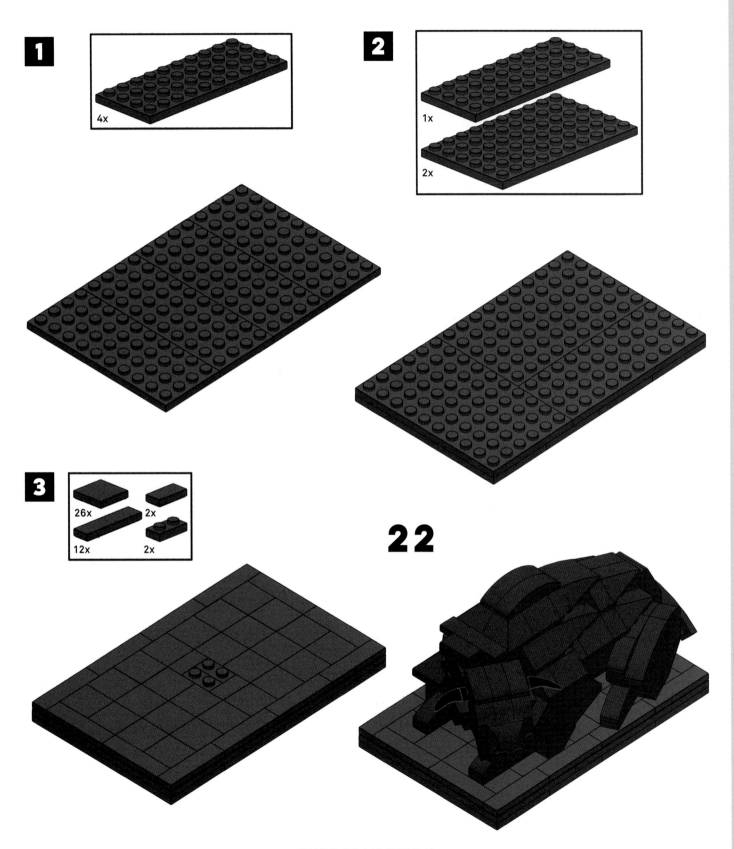

1 4x

2 1x 2x

3 26x 2x 12x 2x

22

GIANT PANDA

Ailuropoda melanoleuca

The giant panda—also known as the panda bear—is simply one of those creatures that's hard not to love. Their two-tone coats and cuddlesome demeanor make them easy to adore. I posed my sculpture paused and looking up to show this reclusive animal's more pensive side.

- While giant pandas do eat fish and small animals, their diet consists primarily of bamboo shoots and leaves, which they spend a good part of the day grinding for digestion using their broad, flat molars.

- Giant pandas are experts at climbing trees and are surprisingly adept swimmers.

- Giant pandas are found only in the misty mountain ranges of central China. Due to their shy nature, they typically avoid people, so their habitat is significantly limited.

- Unfortunately, the giant panda is one of the most endangered species in all of Asia, with only about 1,000 existing in the wild. Efforts to build protective sanctuaries have been made, as well as habitat studies to help conservation programming.

Parts Color Key

■	Black
■	Dark Green
■	Light Bluish Gray
□	White

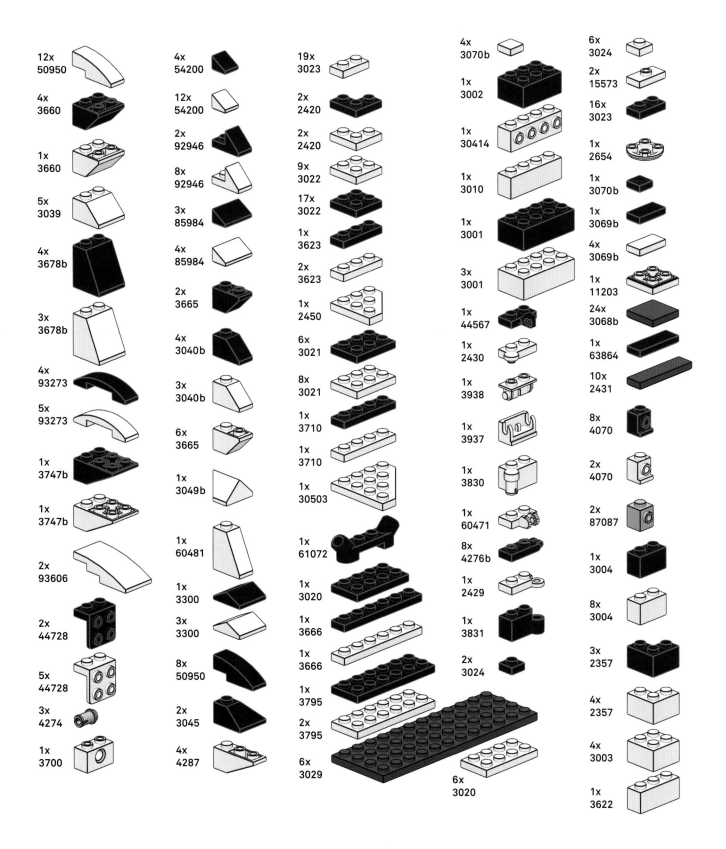

12x 50950
4x 3660
1x 3660
5x 3039
4x 3678b
3x 3678b
4x 93273
5x 93273
1x 3747b
1x 3747b
2x 93606
2x 44728
5x 44728
3x 4274
1x 3700

4x 54200
12x 54200
2x 92946
8x 92946
3x 85984
4x 85984
2x 3665
4x 3040b
3x 3040b
6x 3665
1x 3049b
1x 60481
1x 3300
3x 3300
8x 50950
2x 3045
4x 4287

19x 3023
2x 2420
2x 2420
9x 3022
17x 3022
1x 3623
2x 3623
1x 2450
6x 3021
8x 3021
1x 3710
1x 3710
1x 30503
1x 61072
1x 3020
1x 3666
1x 3666
1x 3795
2x 3795
6x 3029

4x 3070b
1x 3002
1x 30414
1x 3010
1x 3001
3x 3001
1x 44567
1x 2430
1x 3938
1x 3937
1x 3830
1x 60471
8x 4276b
1x 2429
1x 3831
2x 3024

6x 3020

6x 3024
2x 15573
16x 3023
1x 2654
1x 3070b
1x 3069b
4x 3069b
1x 11203
24x 3068b
1x 63864
10x 2431
8x 4070
2x 4070
2x 87087
1x 3004
8x 3004
3x 2357
4x 2357
4x 3003
1x 3622

1

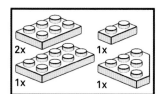

2x 1x
1x 1x

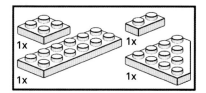

2

1x 1x
1x 1x

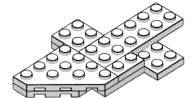

3

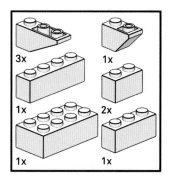

3x 1x
1x 2x
1x 1x

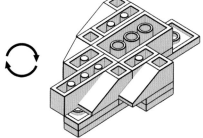

4

3x

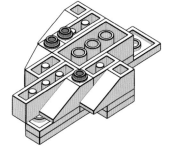

5

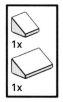

1x
1x

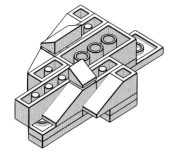

6

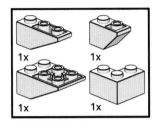

1x 1x
1x 1x

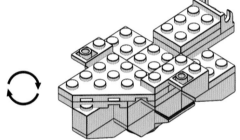

7

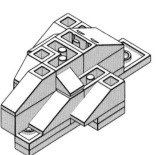

1x

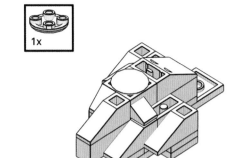

8

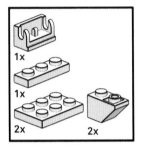

1x
1x
2x 2x

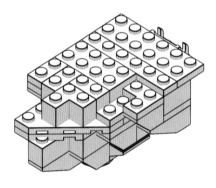

9

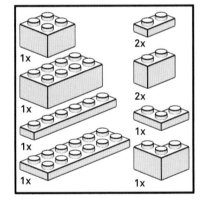

1x 2x

1x 2x

1x 1x

1x 1x

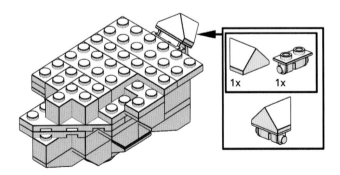

10

1x 1x

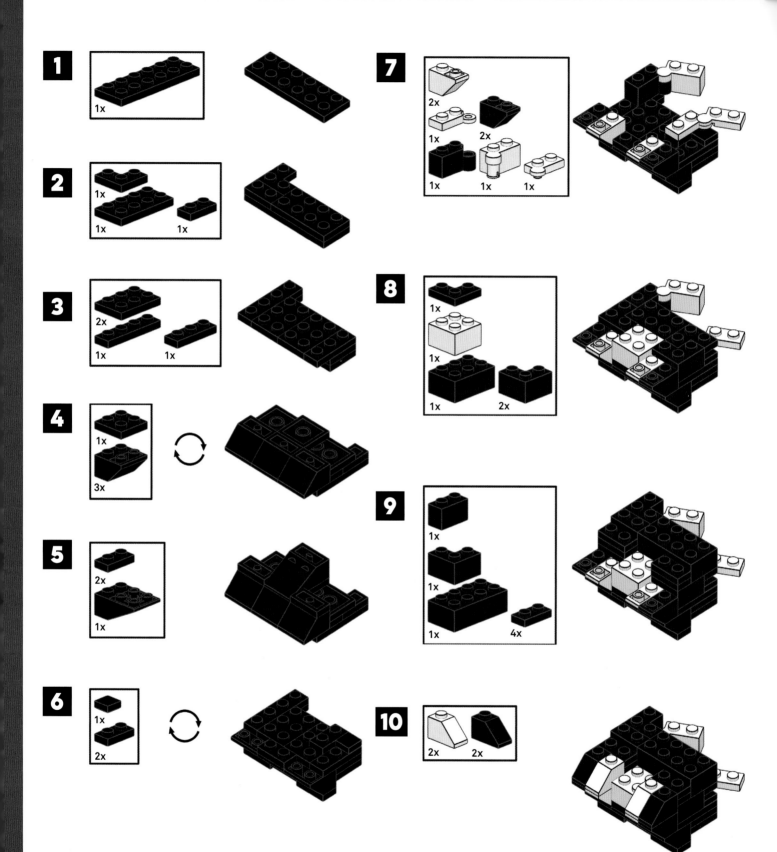

11

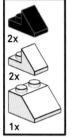 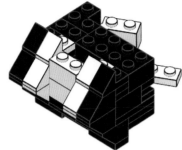

2x

2x

1x

12

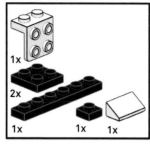 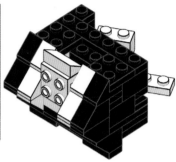

1x

2x

1x   1x   1x

13

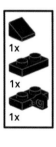 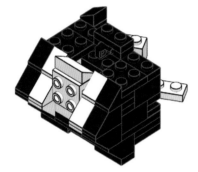

1x

1x

1x

14

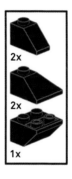 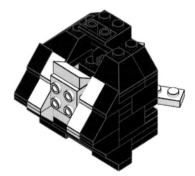

2x

2x

1x

15

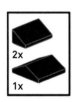

2x

1x

1

1x

2

2x   1x

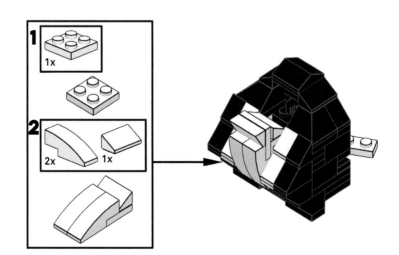

11

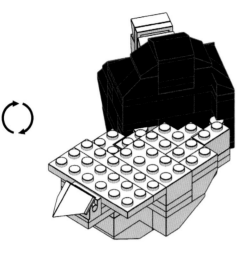

12

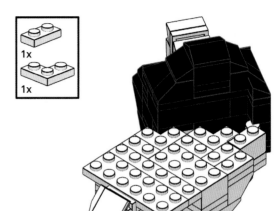

13

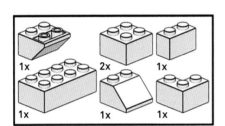

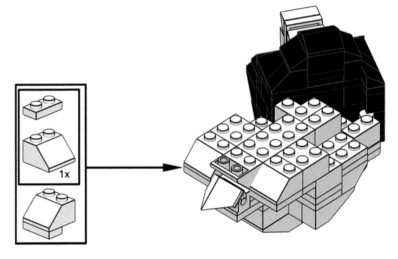

14

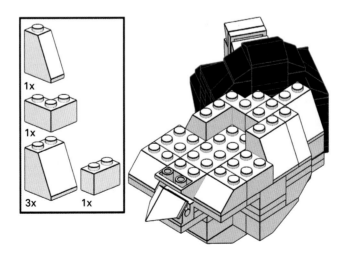

15

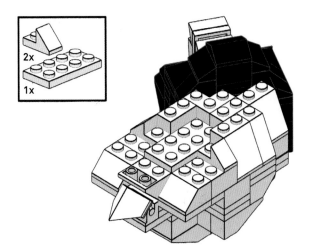

2x
1x

16

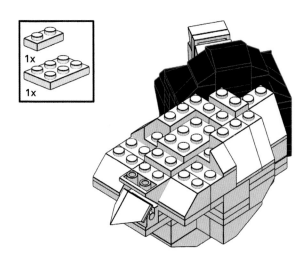

1x
1x

17

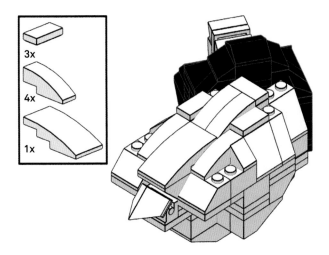

3x
4x
1x

18

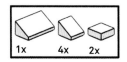

1x
4x
2x

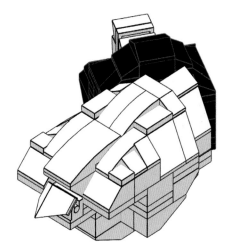

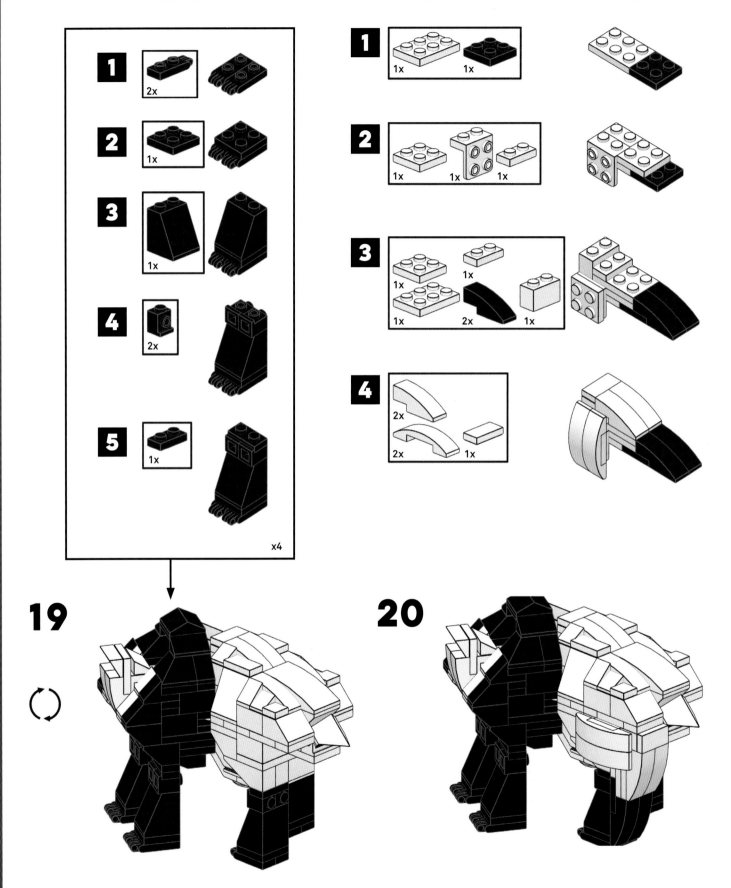

19

20

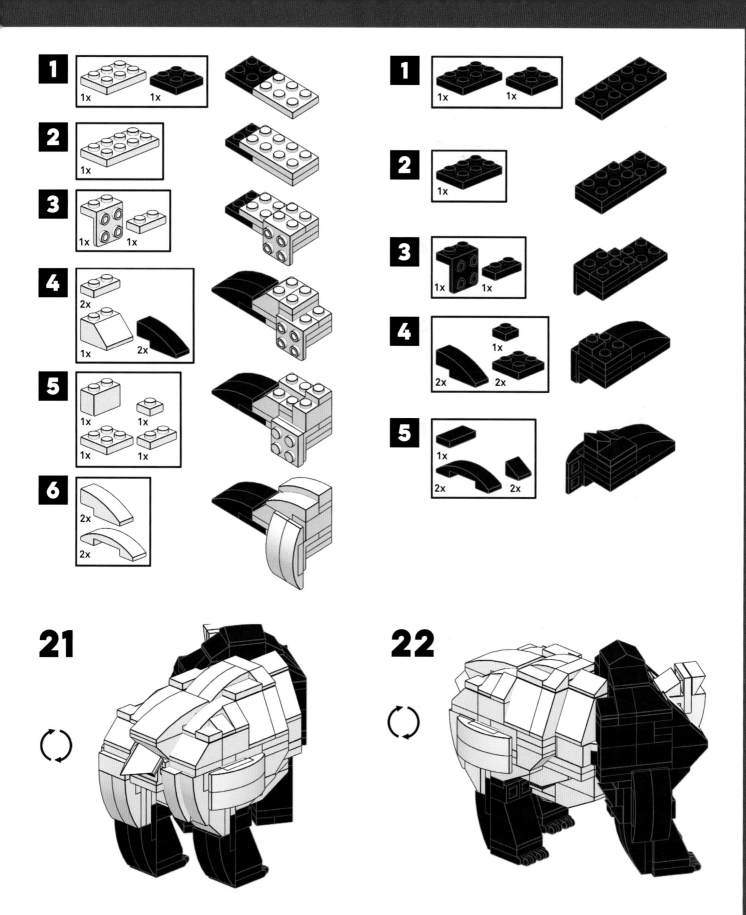

1

1x 1x

2

1x

3

1x 1x

4

2x

2x

5

1x

2x 1x

1

1x

2

1x

1x

1x

3

2x

1x

4

1x 2x 2x

5

1x 2x

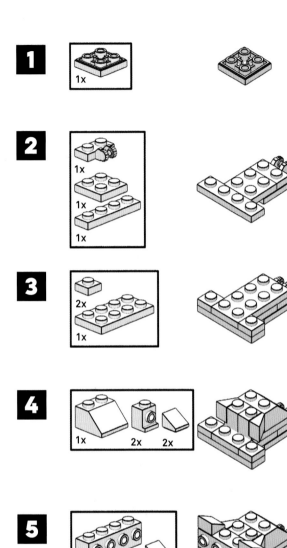

23

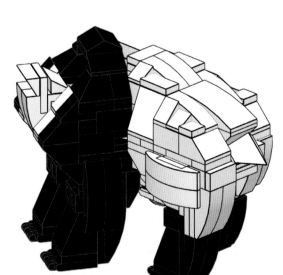

1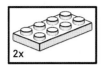

2x

2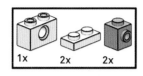

1x 2x 2x

3

2x

4

2x

2x

5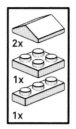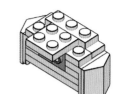

2x

1x

1x

6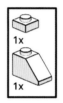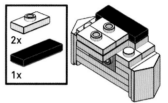

2x

1x

7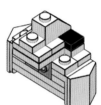

1x

1x

8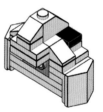

3x

6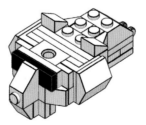

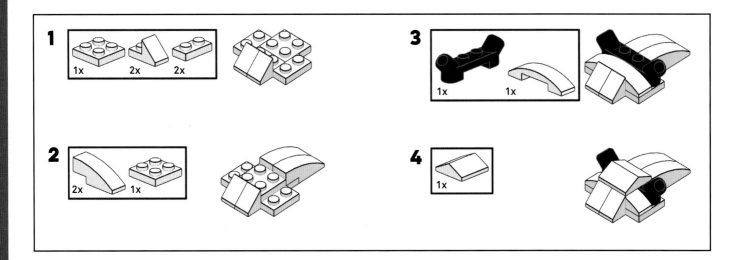

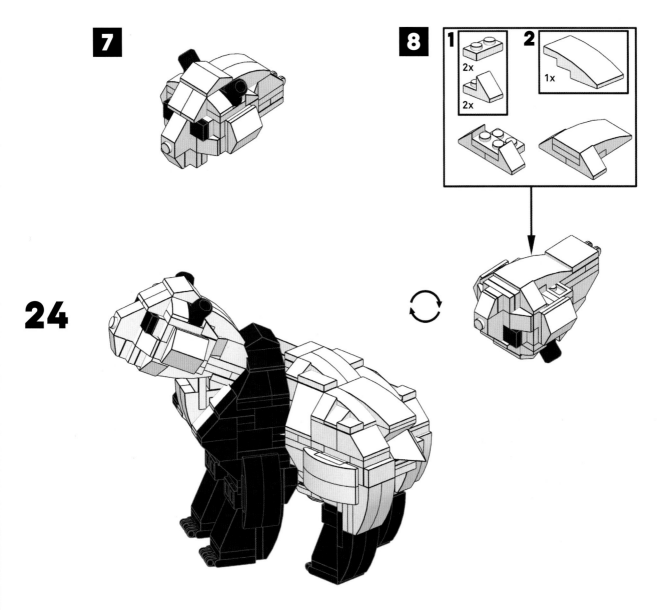

1

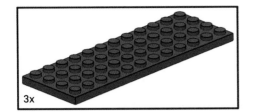

3x

2

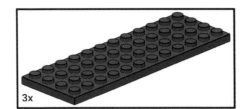

3x

3

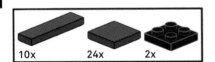

10x   24x   2x

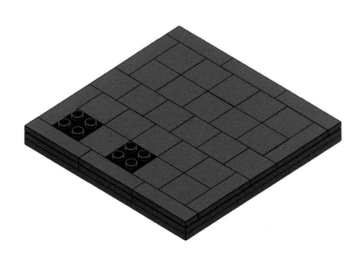

25

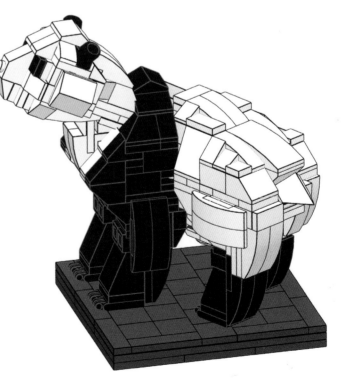

INDIAN RHINOCEROS

Rhinoceros unicornis

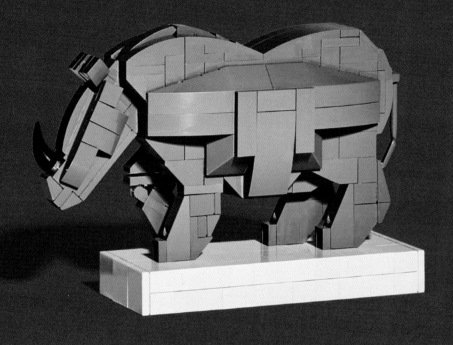

What I find intriguing about the Indian rhinoceros—also called the greater one-horned rhinoceros—is that despite being a 4,400-pound (1,995 kg) herbivore with armor-like skin, they can also be surprisingly maneuverable once set into action. In order to capture the subtle menace of this beast, I built the sculpture with its horn poised and a foreleg raised, as if it were a second away from charging.

- The Indian rhinoceros is found mainly in the grasslands of Nepal and northern India.

- Indian rhinos are known to reach speeds of up to 35 miles per hour (55 km/h) when charging, so running away from one is not an advisable course of action.

- The Indian rhino is a grazing animal that travels along tunnel-like paths through its bushy grassland territory. Using its remarkable prehensile upper lip, it is able to grasp tall grass, fruit, and crops for daily consumption.

- Sadly, the Indian rhino is an endangered species, with only about 2,000 left in the wild.

Parts Color Key

⬛	Black
⬛	Dark bluish gray
⬜	Light bluish gray
⬜	Tan

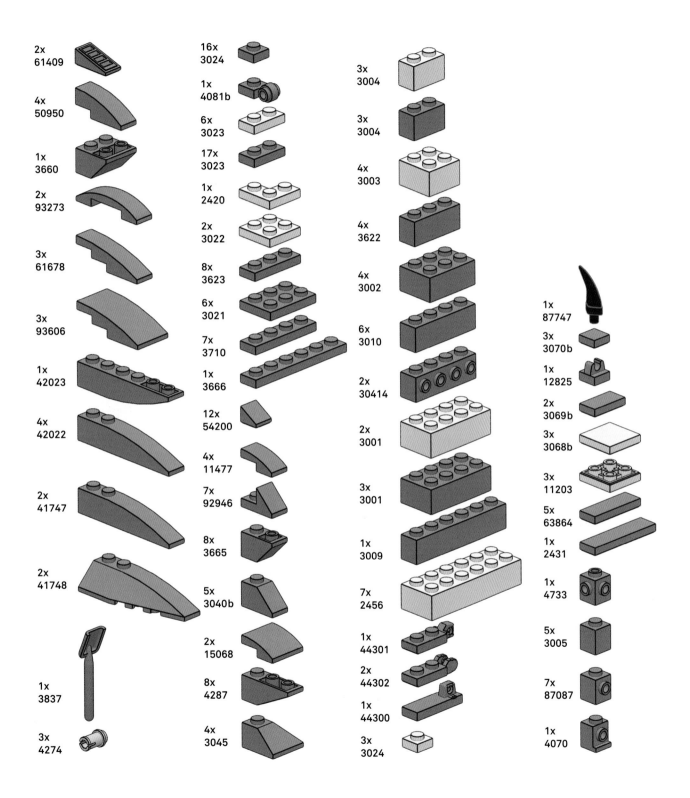

2x 61409

4x 50950

1x 3660

2x 93273

3x 61678

3x 93606

1x 42023

4x 42022

2x 41747

2x 41748

1x 3837

3x 4274

16x 3024

1x 4081b

6x 3023

17x 3023

1x 2420

2x 3022

8x 3623

6x 3021

7x 3710

1x 3666

12x 54200

4x 11477

7x 92946

8x 3665

5x 3040b

2x 15068

8x 4287

4x 3045

3x 3004

3x 3004

4x 3003

4x 3622

4x 3002

6x 3010

2x 30414

2x 3001

3x 3001

1x 3009

7x 2456

1x 44301

2x 44302

1x 44300

3x 3024

1x 87747

3x 3070b

1x 12825

2x 3069b

3x 3068b

3x 11203

5x 63864

1x 2431

1x 4733

5x 3005

7x 87087

1x 4070

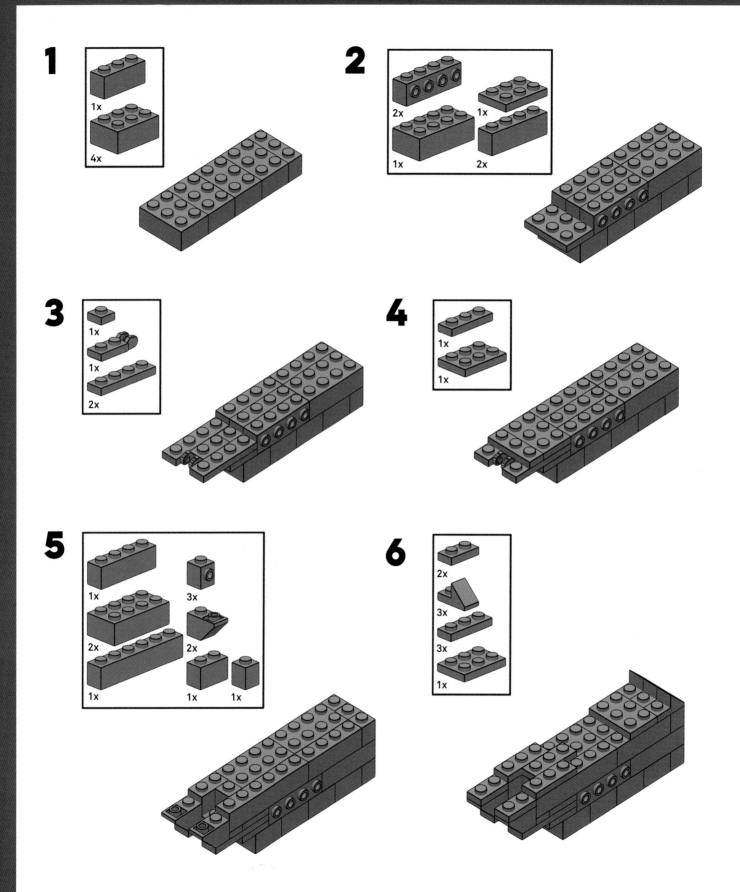

1 1x 4x

2 2x 1x 1x 2x

3 1x 1x 2x

4 1x 1x

5 1x 3x 2x 2x 1x 1x 1x

6 2x 3x 3x 1x

7

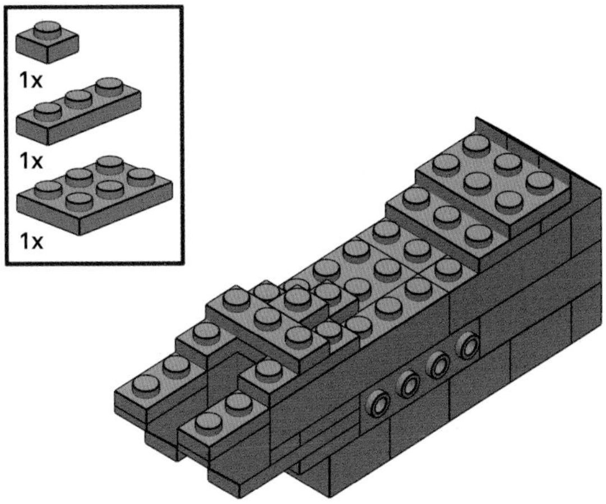

1x
1x
1x

8

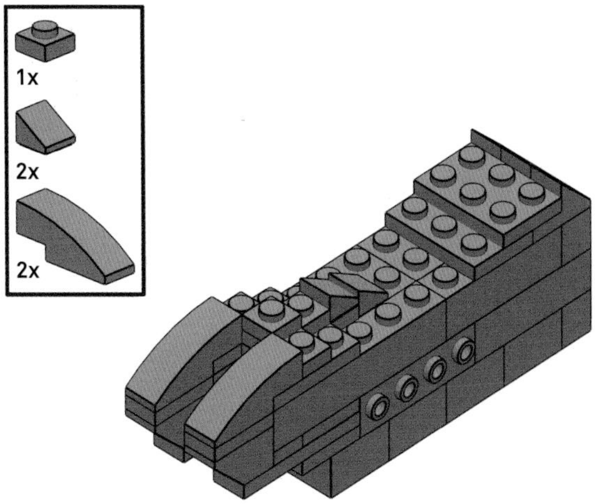

1x
2x
2x

9

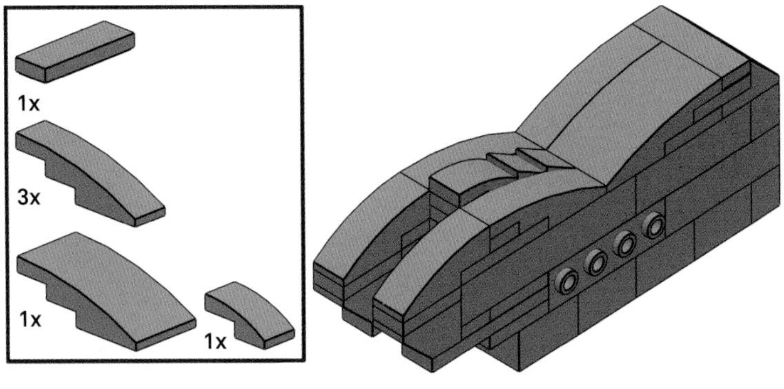

1x
3x
1x
1x

10

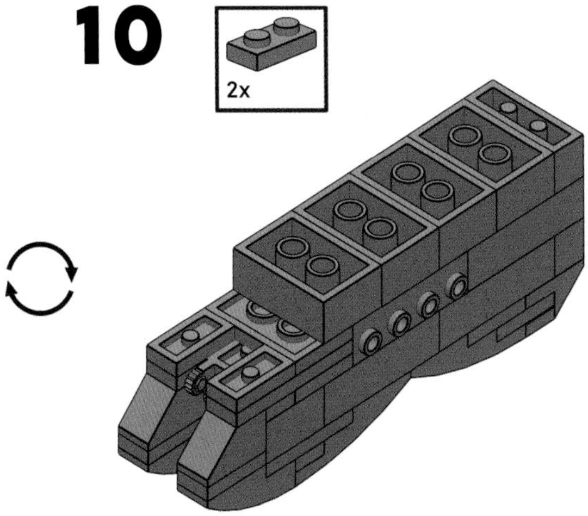

2x

11

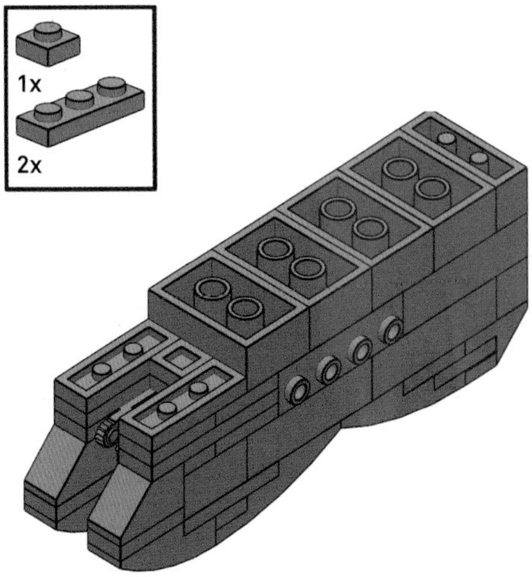

1x
2x

12

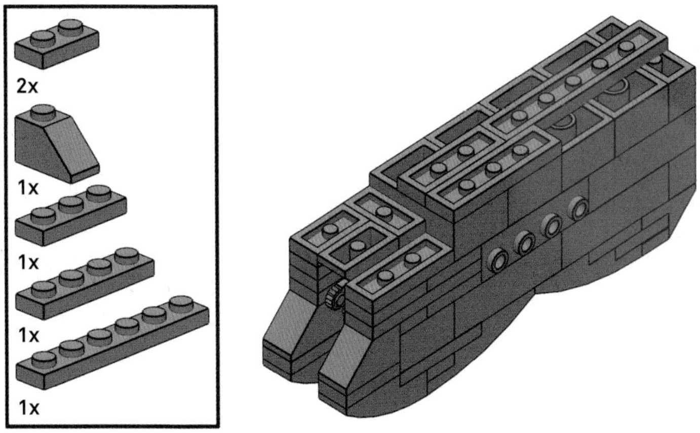

2x
1x
1x
1x
1x

13

1x
1x
1x
1x
2x
2x

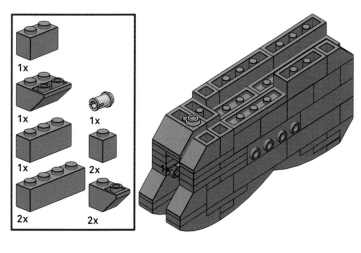

14

1x
1x
1x
1x
3x

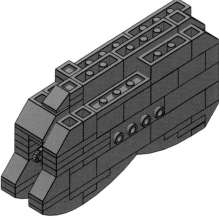

15

1x
1x
1x
1x
1x
1x

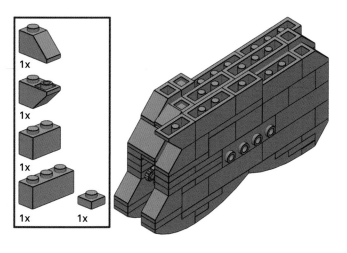

16

1x
1x
2x
1x

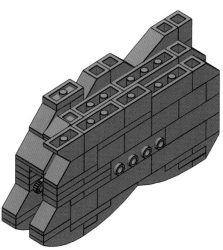

17

2x
1x
1x

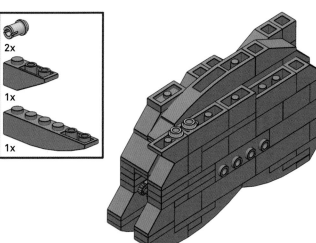

18

19

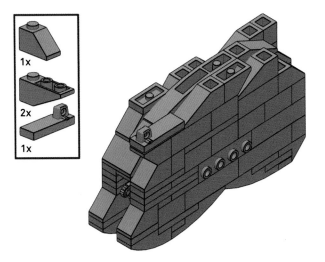

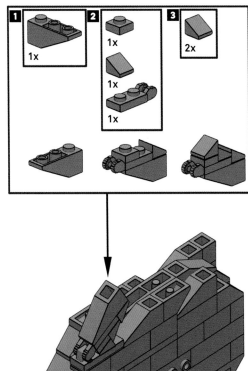

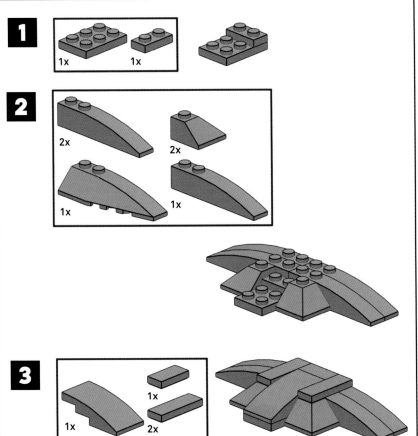

1

1x 1x

2

2x 2x

1x 1x

3

1x 1x

1x 2x

x2

20

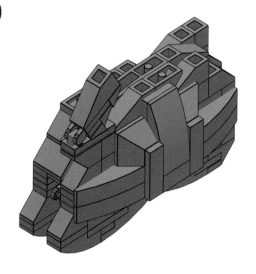

21

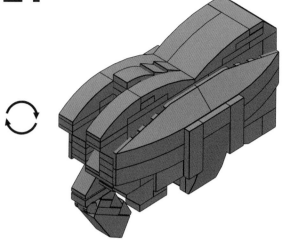

22

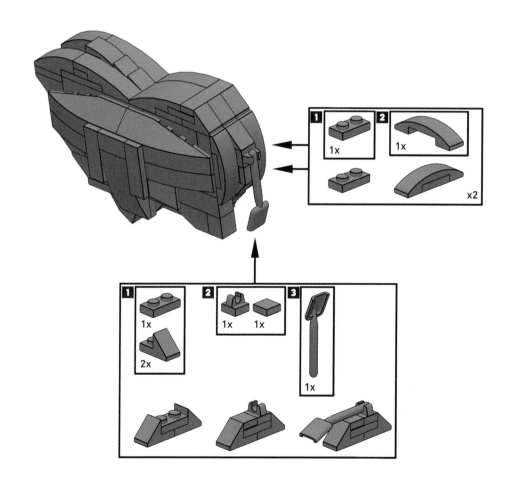

1

1x 1x

2

1x 1x

3

1x

1x 1x

x2

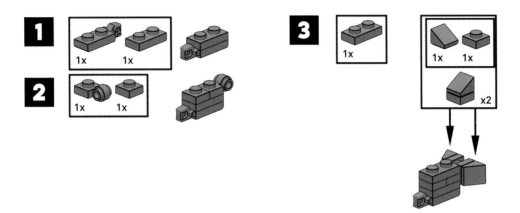

4

2x

5

1x

1x

6

1x

1x 1x

7

1

1x

1x

2

1x

3

1x

1x

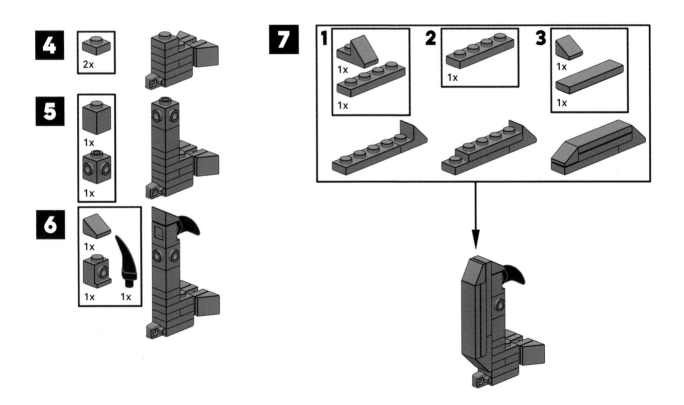

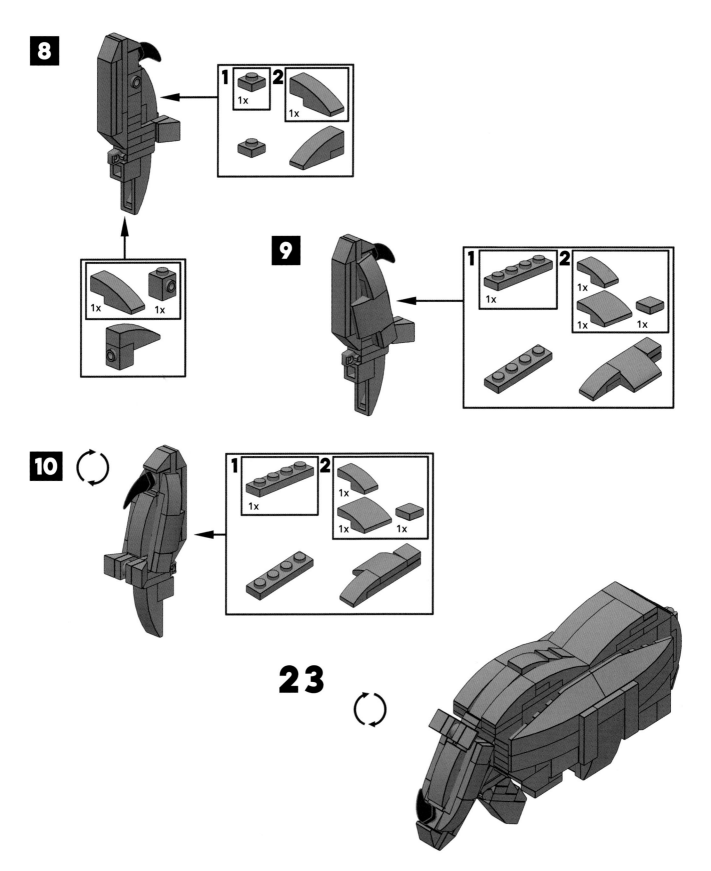

23

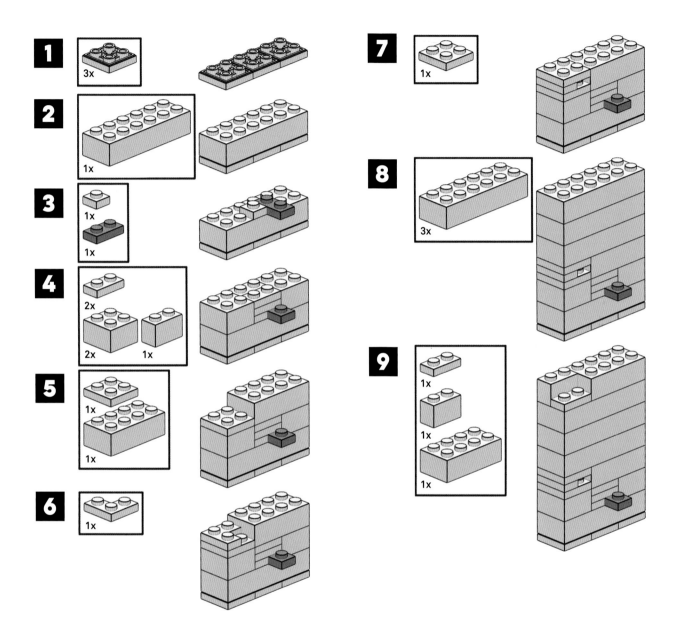

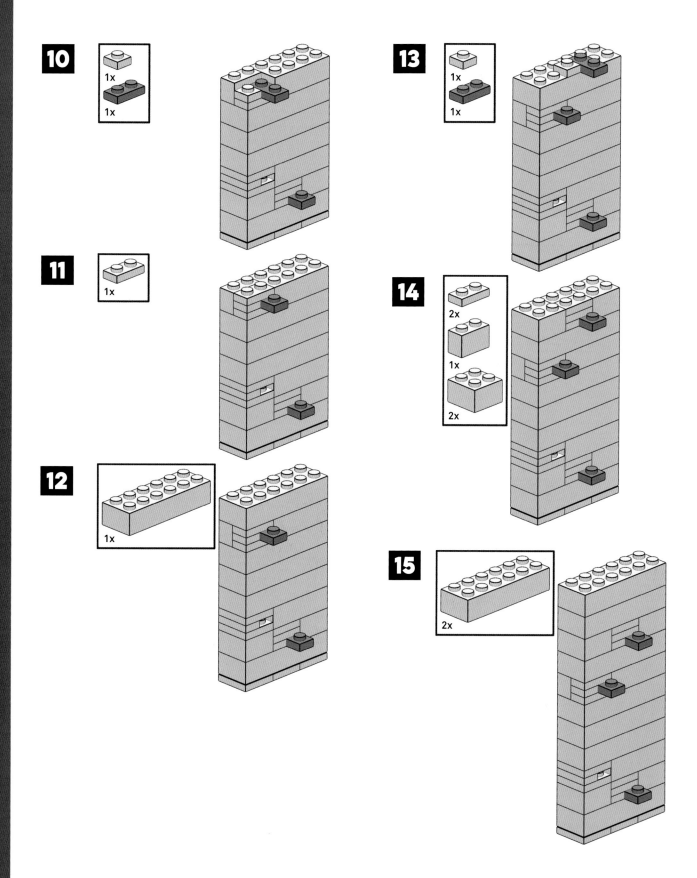

16

3x

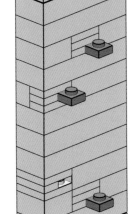

17

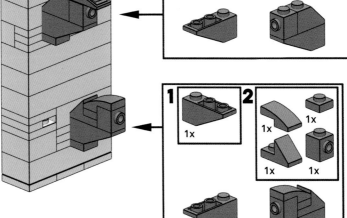

1 1x 2 1x 1x 3 1x 1x

x2

1 1x 2 1x 1x 1x 1x

24

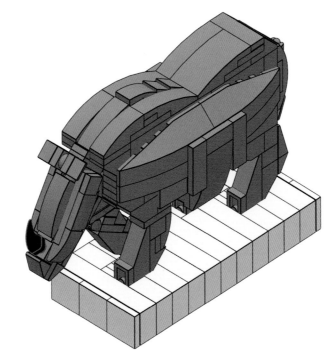

HARP SEAL

Pagophilus groenlandicus

Harp seals spend more time in the water than they do on land, so for this sculpture I decided to take it out of its preferred element and place it on a symbolic patch of ice, raised up on its flippers as if warbling to the sky. I think this piece demonstrates that the harp seal is indeed the delight of the arctic.

- Harp seals love water and can hold their breath for several minutes at a time.

- Young harp seals are born among many on the ice, and their mothers are able to distinguish their own by their unique smell.

- Young harp seals have a uniform white coat that has high commercial demand; as such they have drawn hunters to their breeding grounds for centuries.

Parts Color Key

■	Black
■	Dark bluish gray
■	Light bluish gray
□	White

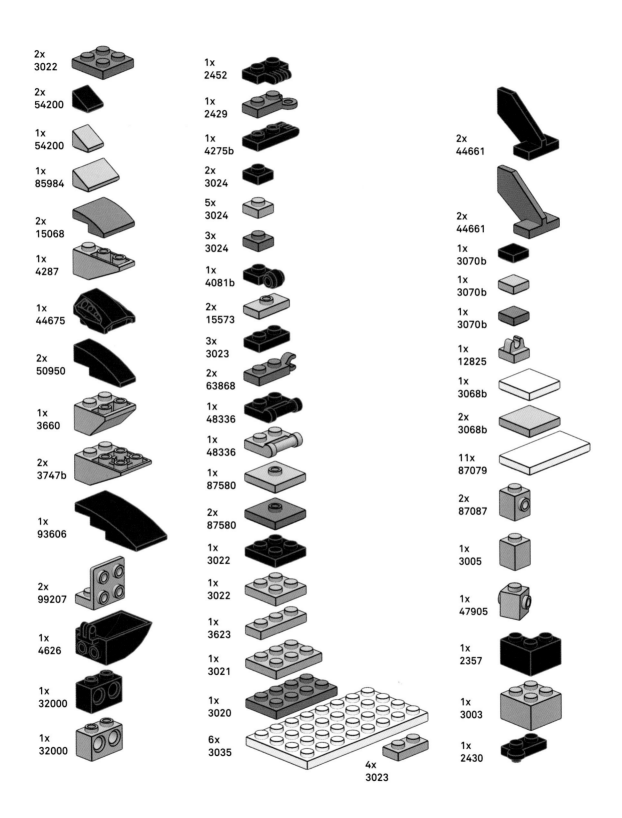

2x 3022
2x 54200
1x 54200
1x 85984
2x 15068
1x 4287
1x 44675
2x 50950
1x 3660
2x 3747b
1x 93606
2x 99207
1x 4626
1x 32000
1x 32000

1x 2452
1x 2429
1x 4275b
2x 3024
5x 3024
3x 3024
1x 4081b
2x 15573
3x 3023
2x 63868
1x 48336
1x 48336
1x 87580
2x 87580
1x 3022
1x 3022
1x 3623
1x 3021
1x 3020
6x 3035
4x 3023

2x 44661
2x 44661
1x 3070b
1x 3070b
1x 3070b
1x 12825
1x 3068b
2x 3068b
11x 87079
2x 87087
1x 3005
1x 47905
1x 2357
1x 3003
1x 2430

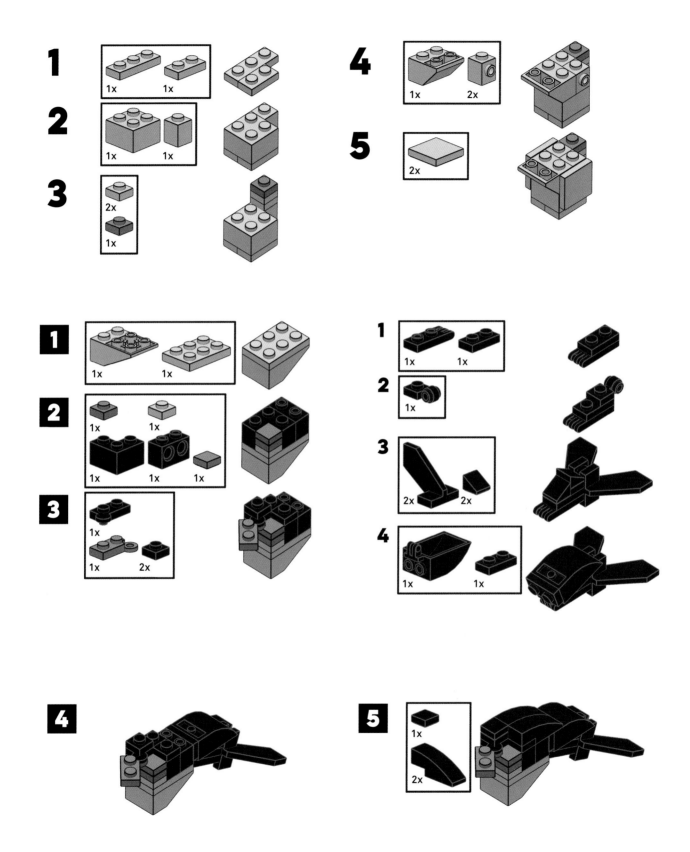

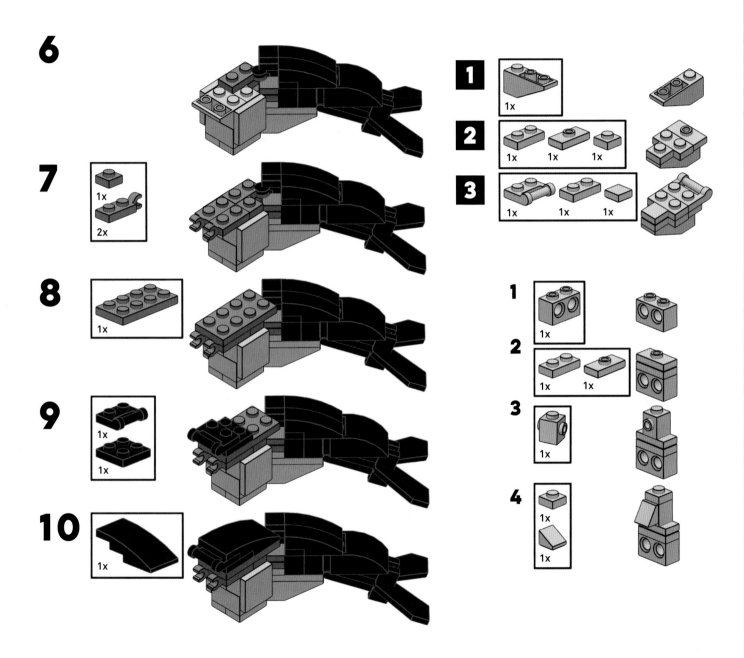

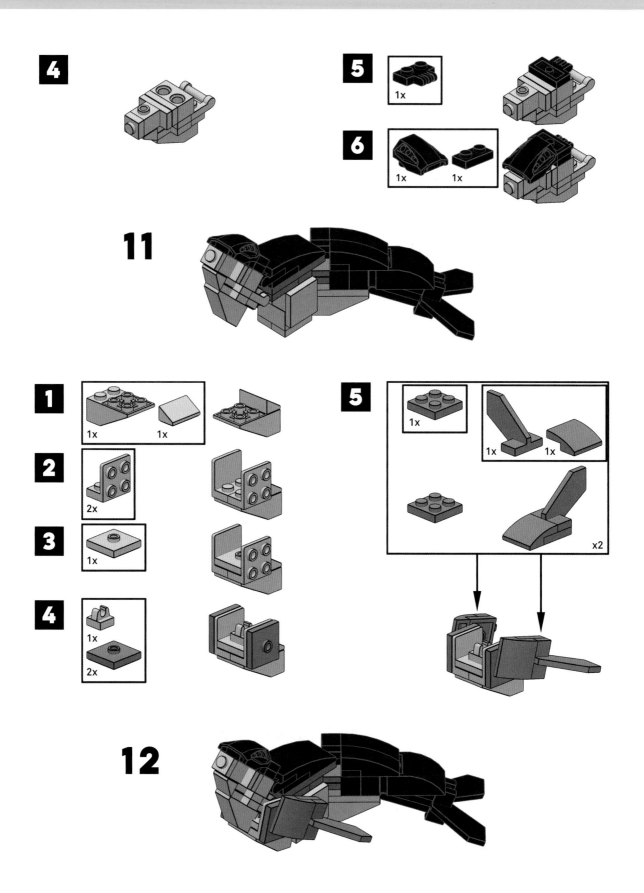

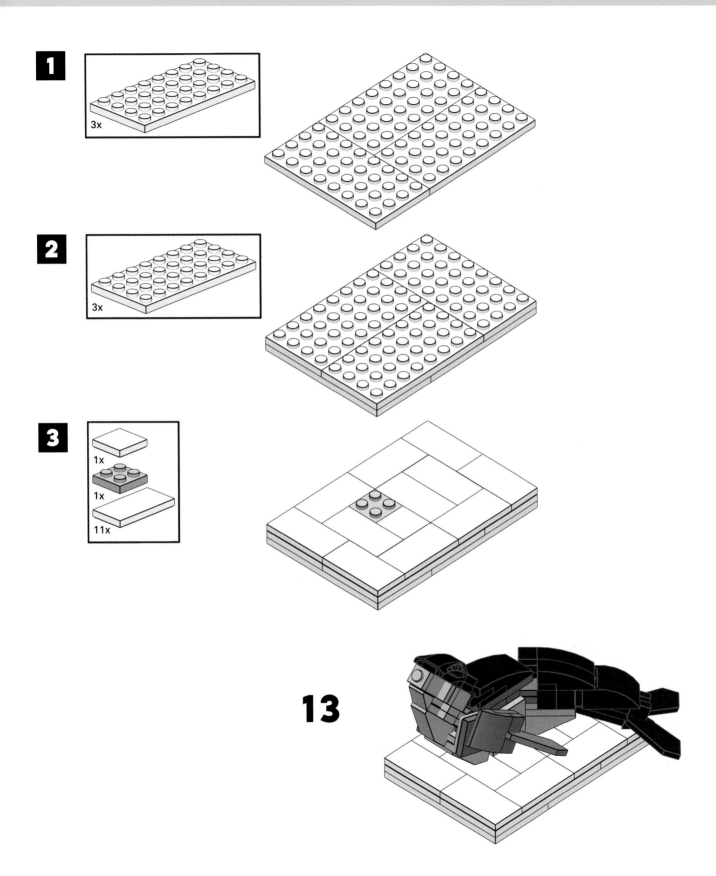

WALRUS

Odobenus rosmarus

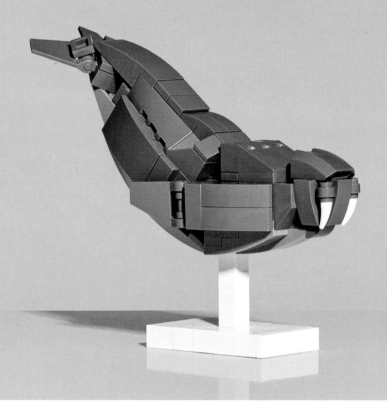

I really enjoyed building this sculpture, especially since I was able to experiment with motion by making it appear to be swimming along a current underwater. Walruses are typically seen as blustering and lethargic, and it was my goal to counter this perception by making my sculpture appear graceful.

- Both male and female walruses grow the characteristic tusks their entire lives; incidentally, these yard-long (1 m) protrusions are actually very large canine teeth.

- Walruses have remarkable thermal control of their heart rate, which is a bonus since they spend most of their time submerged in freezing water.

- The walrus's funny-looking mustache is actually hypersensitive whiskers that allow them to sense food underwater.

- Walruses are considered a threatened species despite laws that restrict hunting.

Parts Color Key

■	Dark bluish gray
■	Dark tan
■	Light bluish gray
□	White

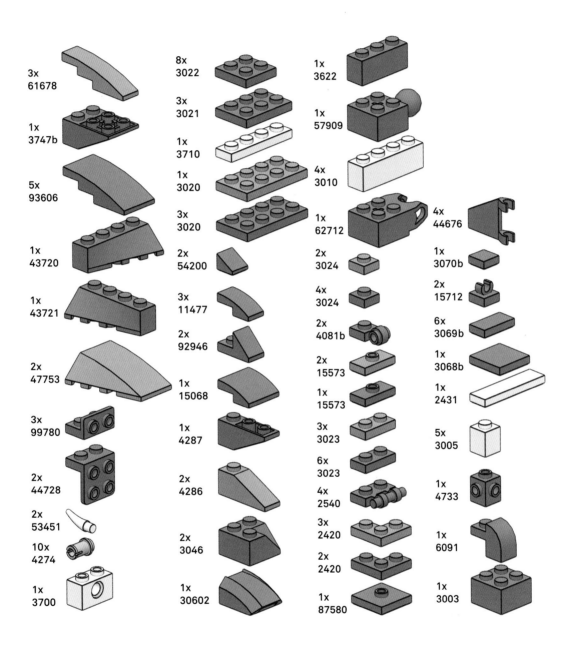

3x
61678

1x
3747b

5x
93606

1x
43720

1x
43721

2x
47753

3x
99780

2x
44728

2x
53451

10x
4274

1x
3700

8x
3022

3x
3021

1x
3710

1x
3020

3x
3020

2x
54200

3x
11477

2x
92946

1x
15068

1x
4287

2x
4286

2x
3046

1x
30602

1x
3622

1x
57909

4x
3010

1x
62712

2x
3024

4x
3024

2x
4081b

2x
15573

1x
15573

3x
3023

6x
3023

4x
2540

3x
2420

2x
2420

1x
87580

4x
44676

1x
3070b

2x
15712

6x
3069b

1x
3068b

1x
2431

5x
3005

1x
4733

1x
6091

1x
3003

1

1x **1x**

2

1x **1x**

3

1x **1x** **1x**

4

1x **1x**

5

1x

6

2x

7

1x
1x

8

3x
1x

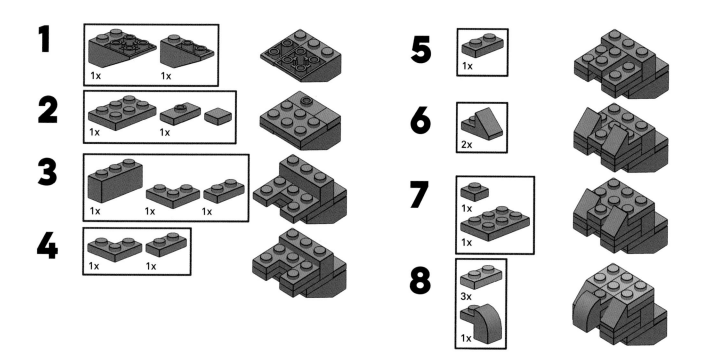

9

1 **2x**

2 **1x**

3 **2x**

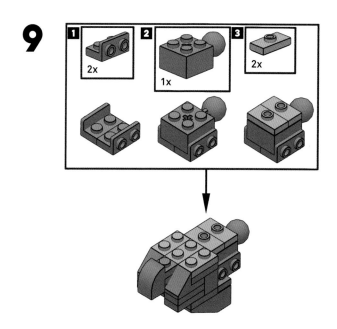

10

1 2x 1x **2** 1x 1x **3** 3x

11

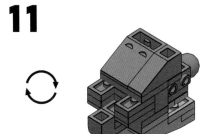

1
2x

2
1x

3
2x 1x

4
3x

5
2x 1x

12

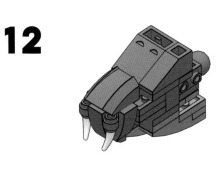

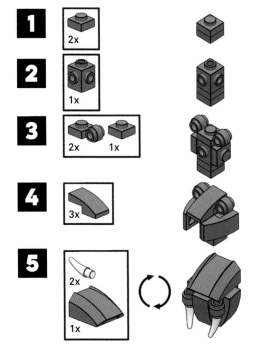

1

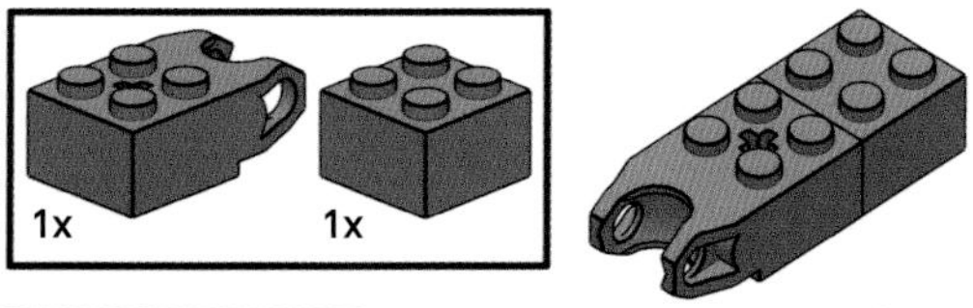

1x 1x

2

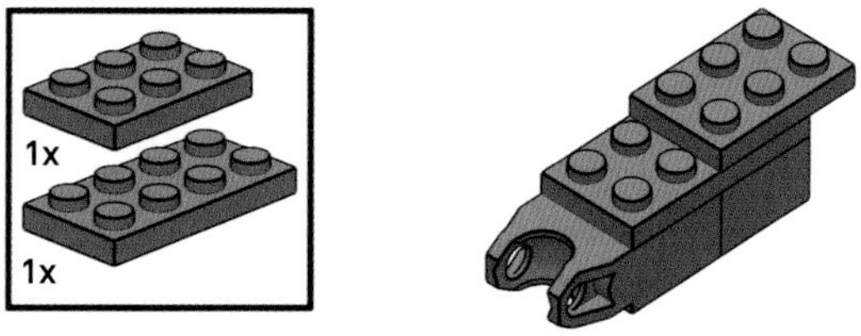

1x

1x

3

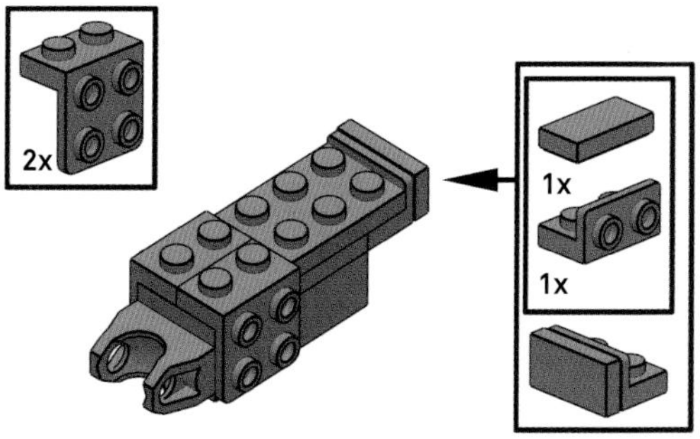

2x

1x

1x

4

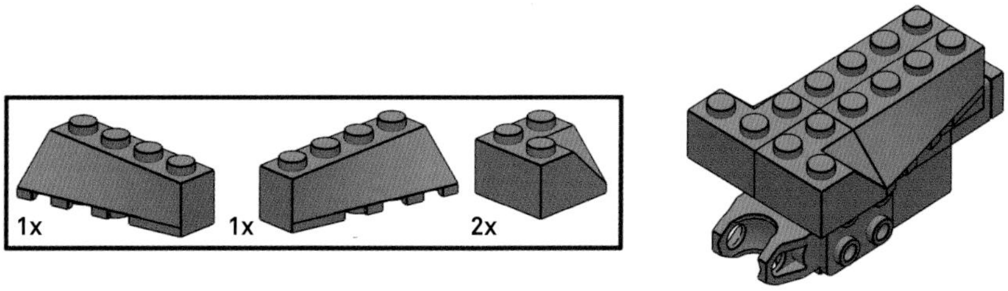

1x 1x 2x

5

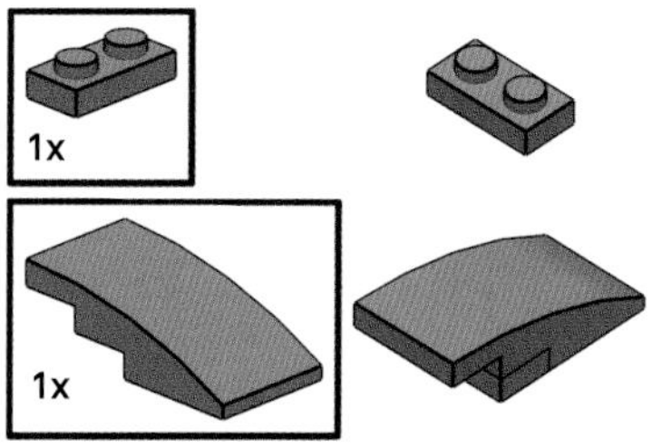

1x

1x

6

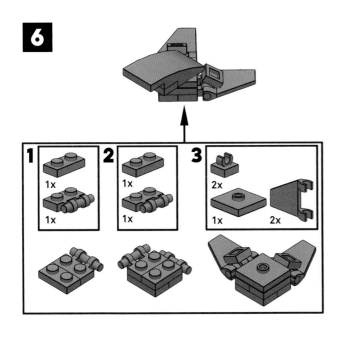

1 1x 1x

2 1x 1x

3 2x 1x 2x

7

1x 1x

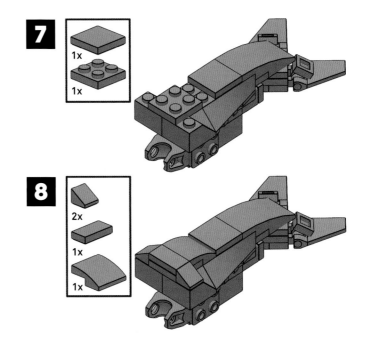

8

2x 1x 1x

9

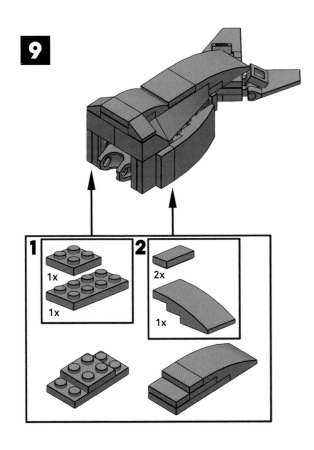

1 1x 1x

2 2x 1x

10

8x

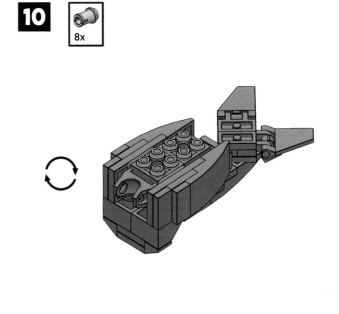

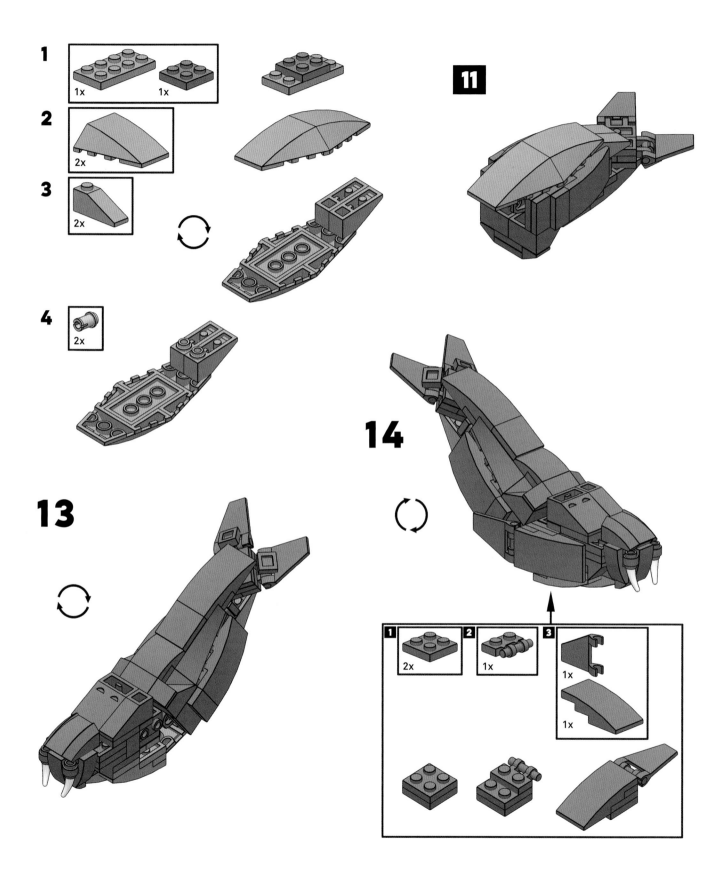

15

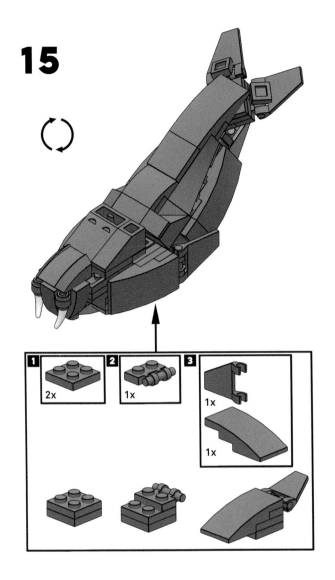

1 2x	**2** 1x	**3** 1x 1x

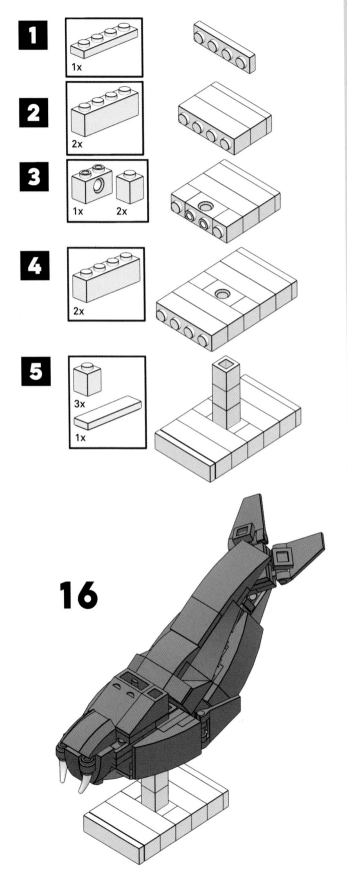

1 1x

2 2x

3 1x 2x

4 2x

5 3x 1x

16

WHITE-TAILED JACKRABBIT

Lepus townsendii

Despite its name, the white-tailed jackrabbit isn't actually a rabbit—it's a hare—and as such it has slightly different features than its smaller, slower cousin. It was important for me to create this fast and furtive creature in a moment of pure motion to capture its sense of nimbleness, almost as if it were evading a predator.

- Not surprisingly, jackrabbits are a main source of prey for many other beasts in the wild, including coyotes, badgers, and bobcats—if they can be caught, that is.

- Jackrabbits are voracious eaters, making them a nuisance to agriculturists across the continent.

- Jackrabbits are prolific breeders. Their numbers remain stable and the species is not in need of protection.

Parts Color Key

	Green
	Light bluish gray
	Reddish brown
	White

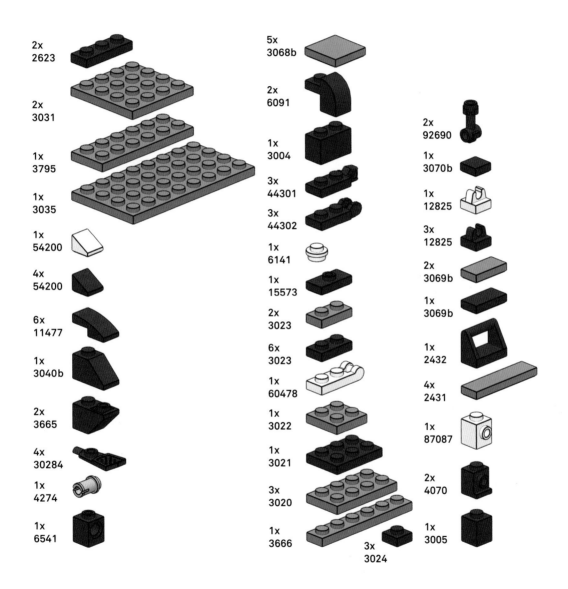

2x
2623

2x
3031

1x
3795

1x
3035

1x
54200

4x
54200

6x
11477

1x
3040b

2x
3665

4x
30284

1x
4274

1x
6541

5x
3068b

2x
6091

1x
3004

3x
44301

3x
44302

1x
6141

1x
15573

2x
3023

6x
3023

1x
60478

1x
3022

1x
3021

3x
3020

1x
3666

3x
3024

2x
92690

1x
3070b

1x
12825

3x
12825

2x
3069b

1x
3069b

1x
2432

4x
2431

1x
87087

2x
4070

1x
3005

1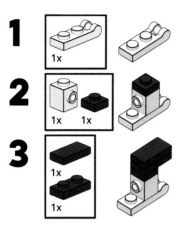

2

3

4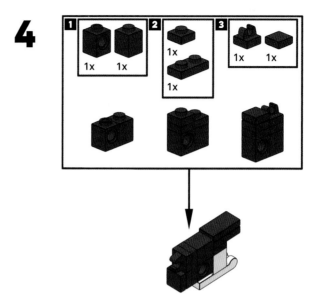

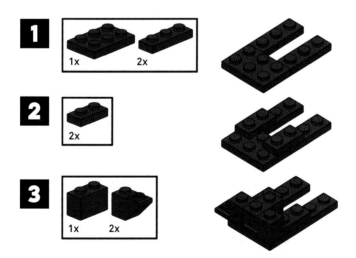

4

4x
2x

5

1x
2x 1x

6

1x
2x
1x

5

6

1
1x
1x

2
1x

3
2x

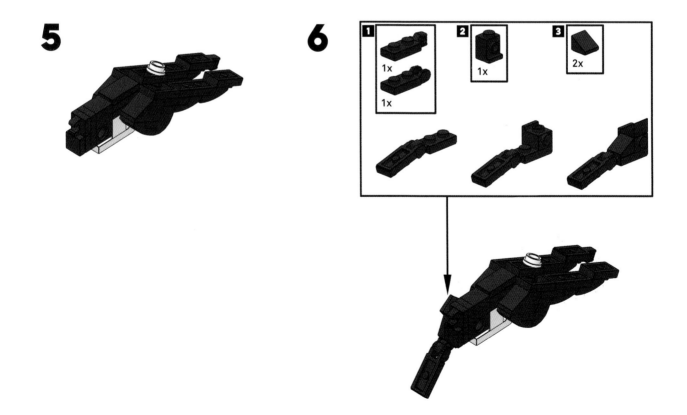

7

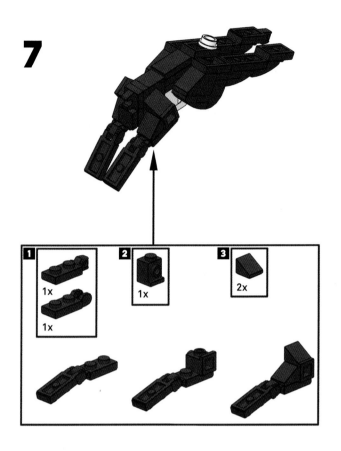

1
1x
1x

2
1x

3
2x

1
1x

2
1x 1x

3
1x 1x

4
2x

5
2x 1x

x2

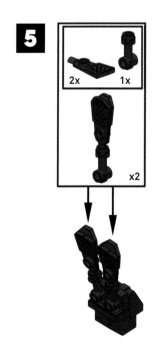

8

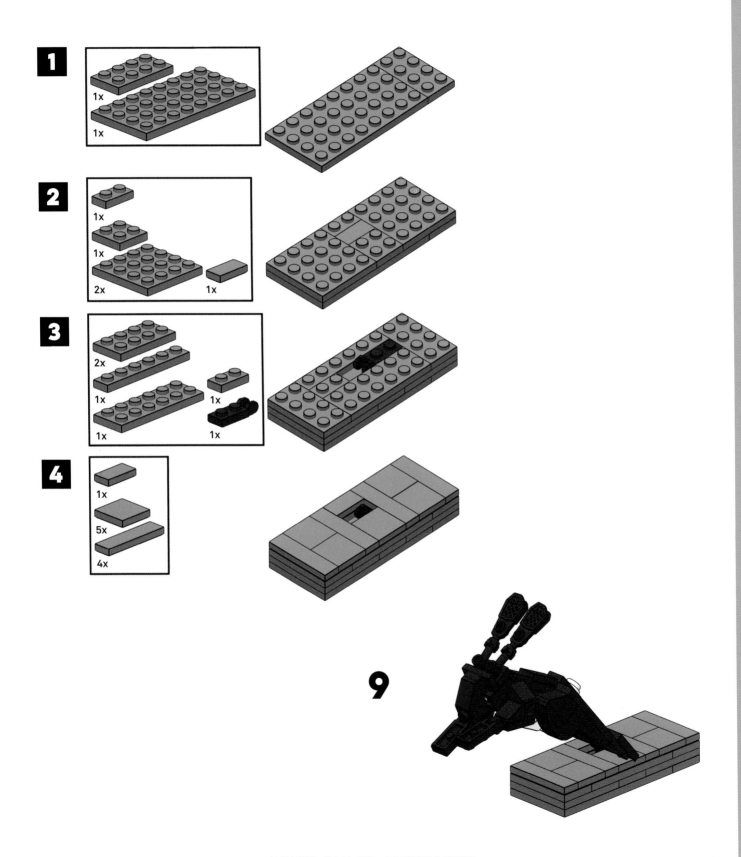

1

1x
1x

2

1x
1x
2x
1x

3

2x
1x
1x
1x
1x

4

1x
5x
4x

9

KERMODE BEAR

Ursus americanus kermodei

The Kermode bear, also known as the spirit bear or Moksgm'ol by the Tsimshian peoples of the Pacific northwest coast, captured my interest the moment I found out about them. They are typically described as having white fur, though in pictures the fur actually has a creamy off-white hue, so to avoid this sculpture being mistaken for a polar bear, I decided to build it with a warmer, tan-colored coat.

- Kermode bears are not albino—they're actually black bears. Their uncharacteristic fur is the result of a recessive gene passed on to them by both parents.

- Princess Royal Island and Gribbell Island in British Columbia have the largest population of Kermode bears in Canada.

- Kermode bears can live to be 25 years old and reach weights of nearly 300 pounds (136 kg).

Parts Color Key

- Dark green
- Light bluish gray
- Tan

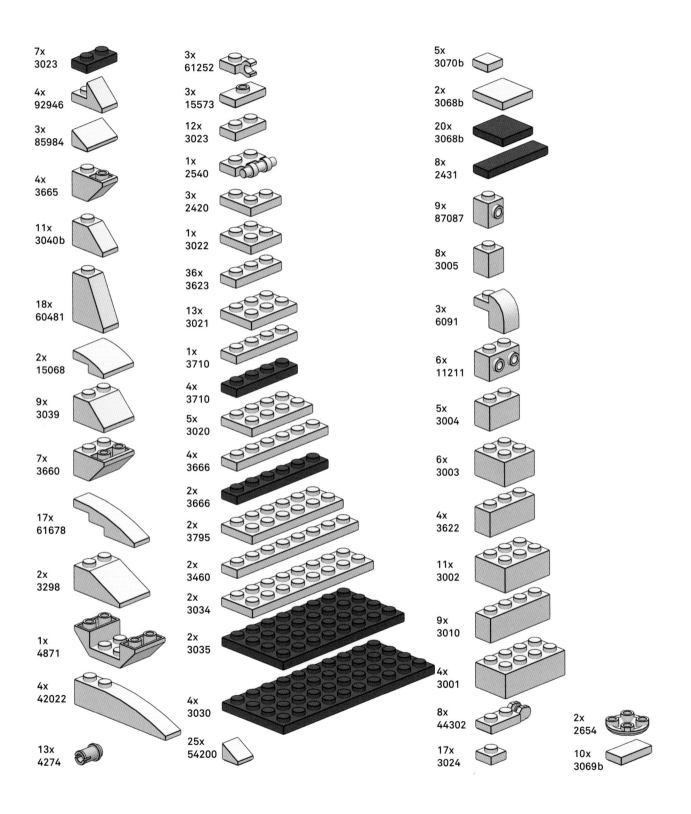

7x
3023

4x
92946

3x
85984

4x
3665

11x
3040b

18x
60481

2x
15068

9x
3039

7x
3660

17x
61678

2x
3298

1x
4871

4x
42022

13x
4274

3x
61252

3x
15573

12x
3023

1x
2540

3x
2420

1x
3022

36x
3623

13x
3021

1x
3710

4x
3710

5x
3020

4x
3666

2x
3666

2x
3795

2x
3460

2x
3034

2x
3035

4x
3030

25x
54200

5x
3070b

2x
3068b

20x
3068b

8x
2431

9x
87087

8x
3005

3x
6091

6x
11211

5x
3004

6x
3003

4x
3622

11x
3002

9x
3010

4x
3001

8x
44302

17x
3024

2x
2654

10x
3069b

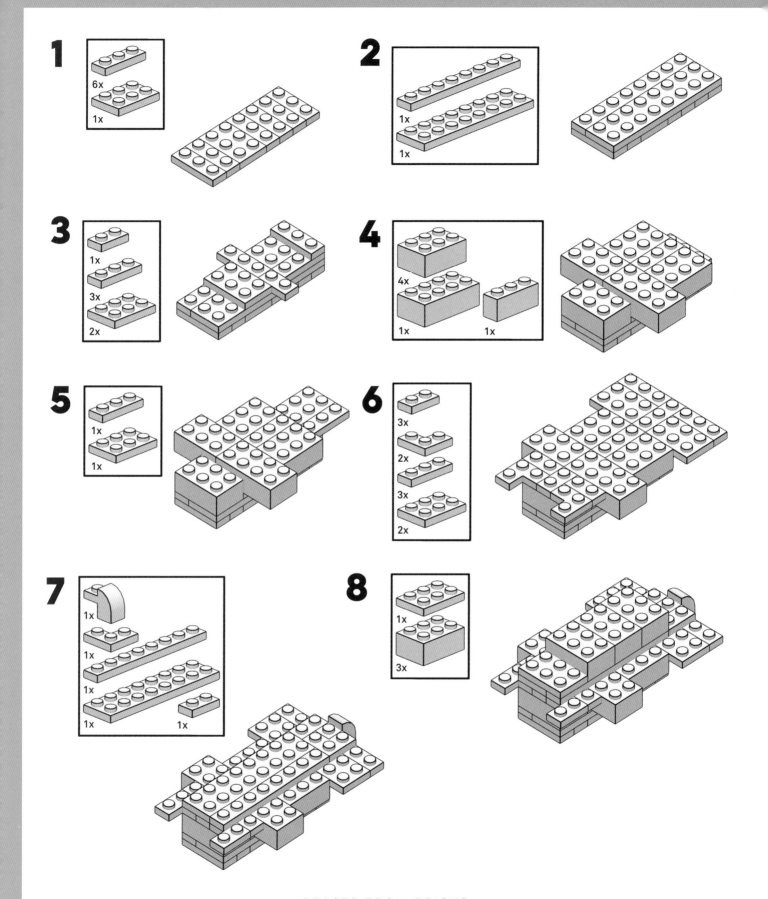

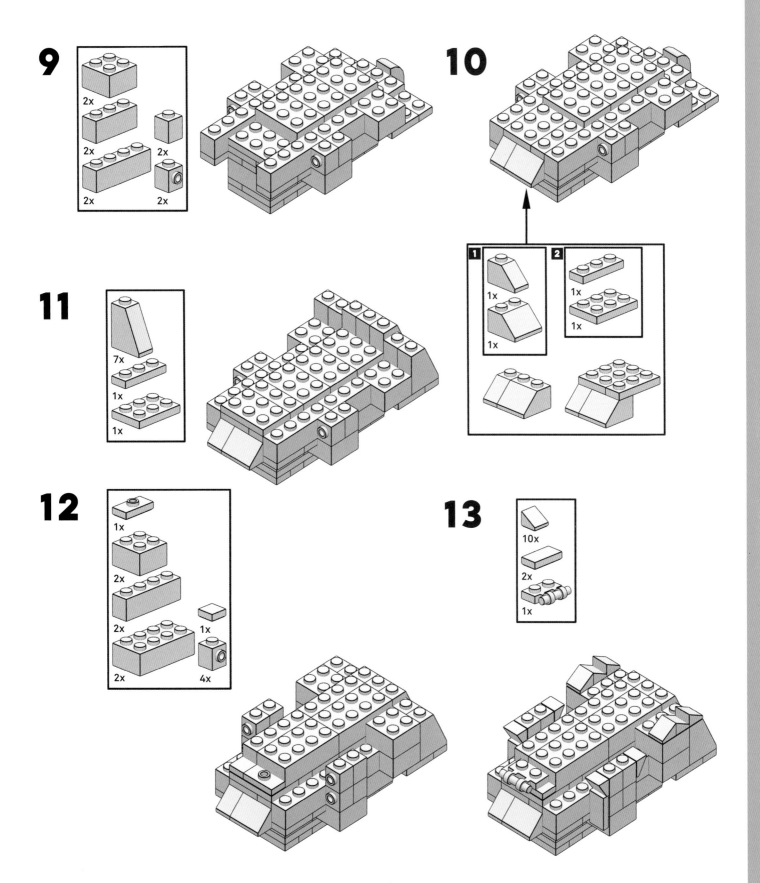

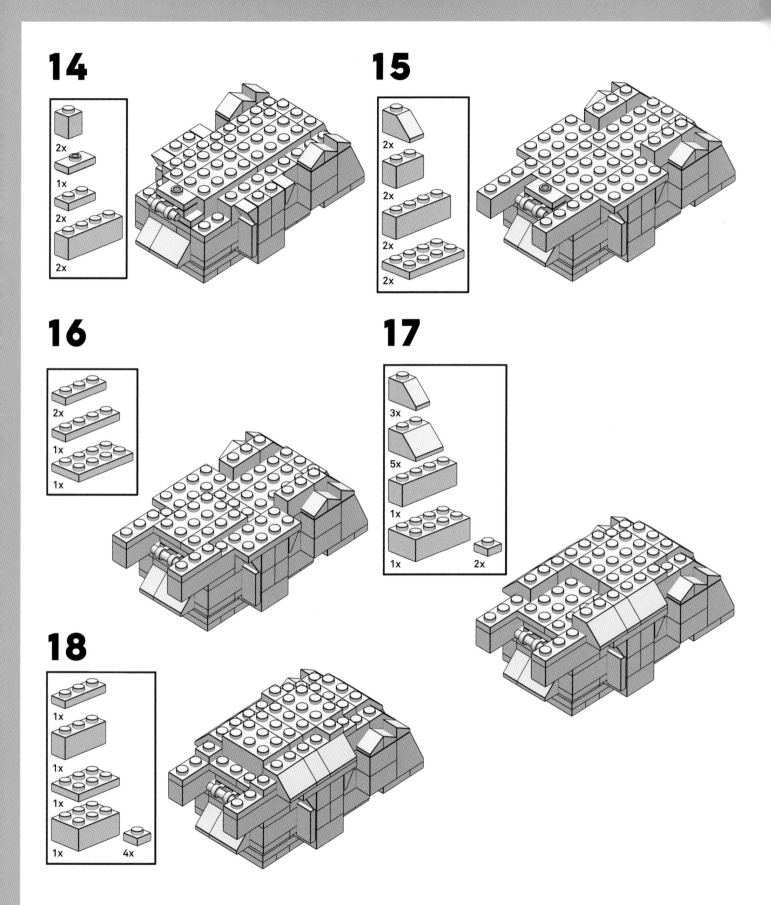

14

2x
1x
2x
2x

15

2x
2x
2x
2x

16

2x
1x
1x

17

3x
5x
1x
1x
2x

18

1x
1x
1x
1x
4x

19

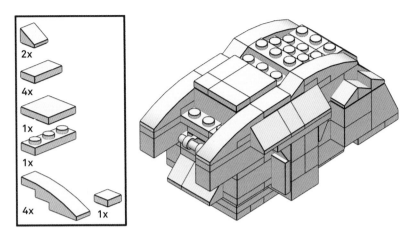

2x

4x

1x

1x

4x

1x

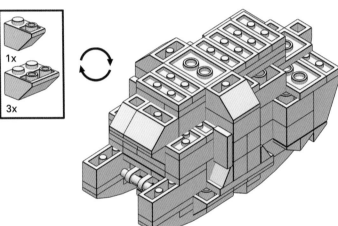

20

3x

3x

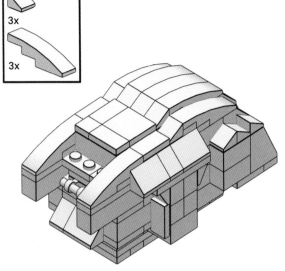

21

1x

3x

22

4x

1x

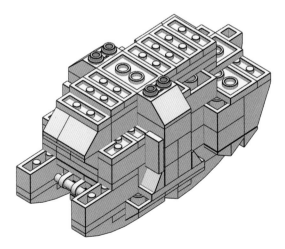

23

24

2x

2x

1 1x

2 1x

1x

1 1x

2 1x

1x

3 1x

3x

4 2x

5 1x

2x

1 1x

1x

2x

2 2x

1x 1x

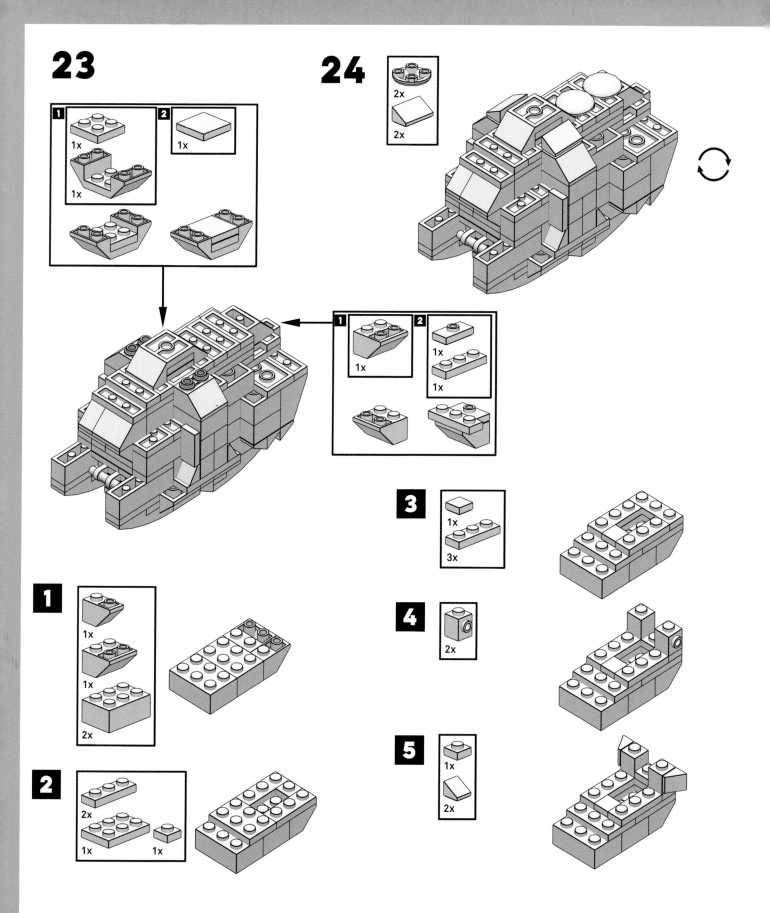

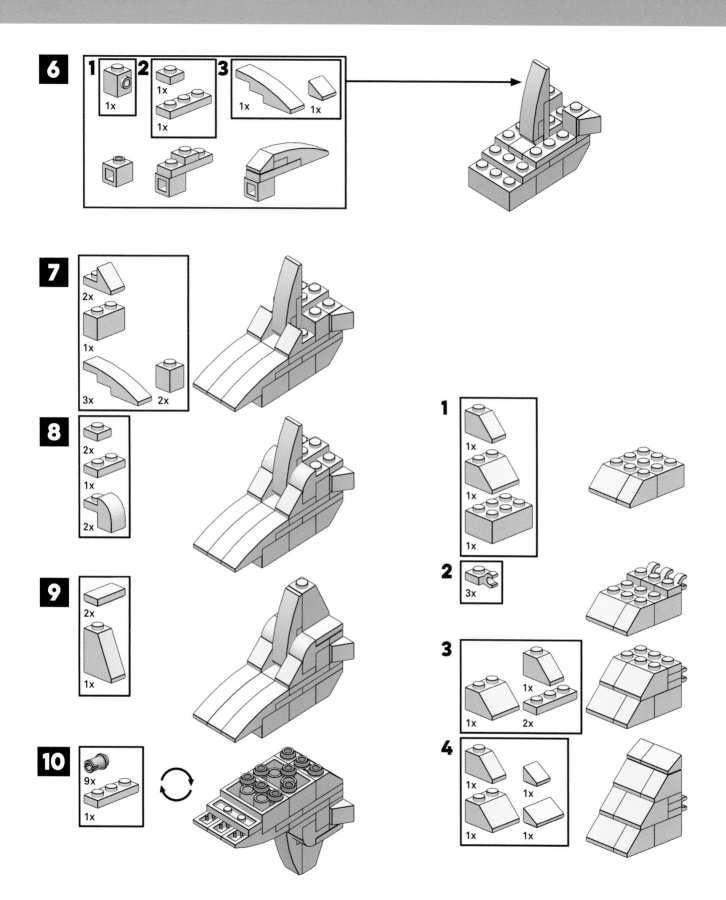

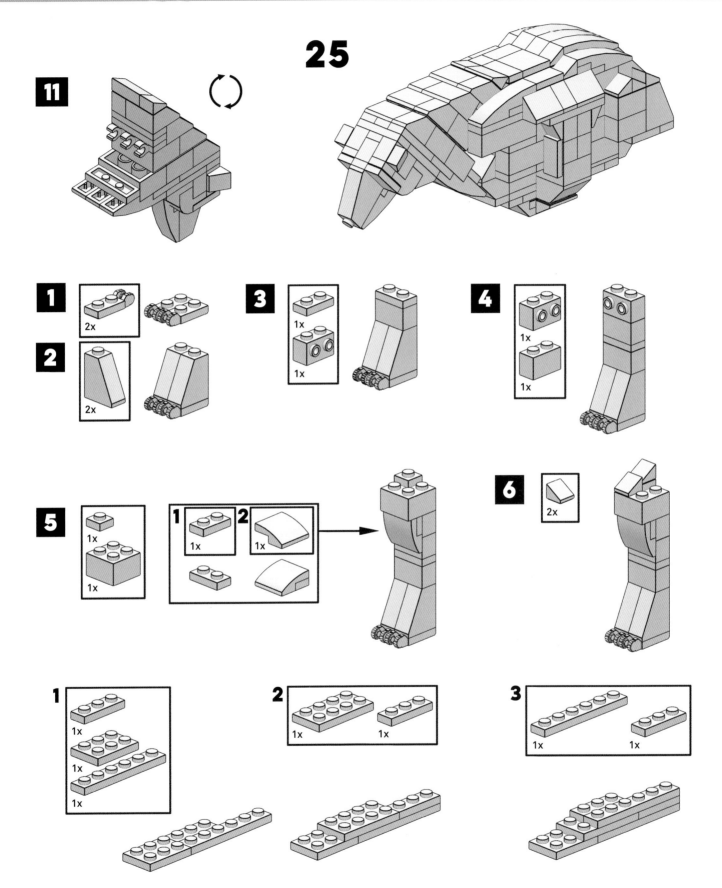

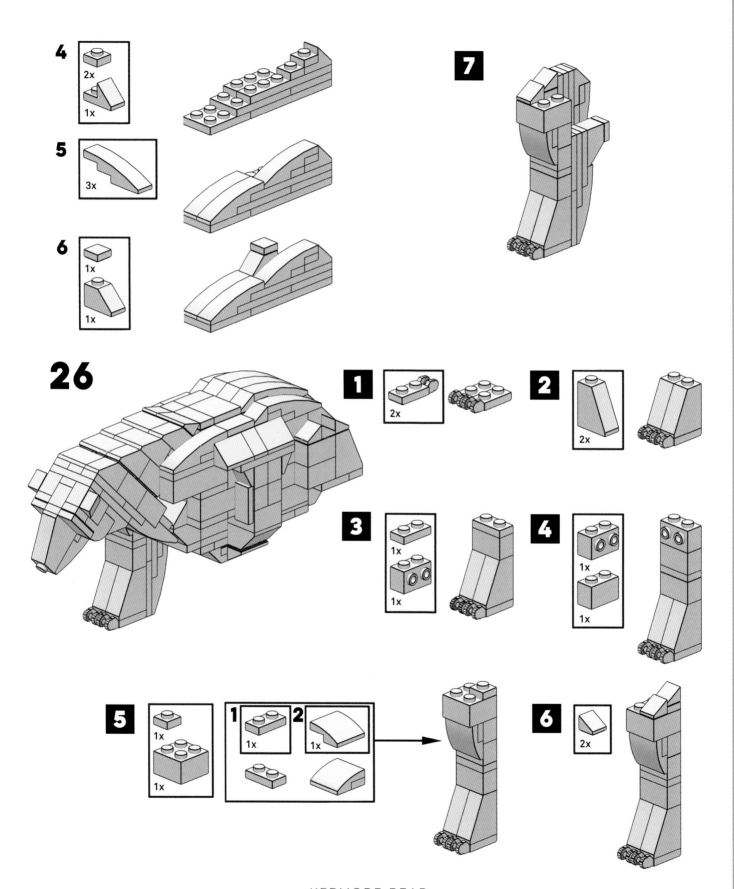

1

1x

1x

1x

2

1x   1x

3

1x

1x

4

2x

1x

5

3x

6

1x

1x

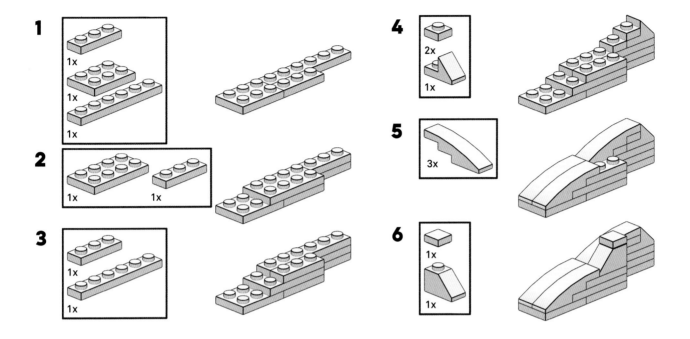

7

27

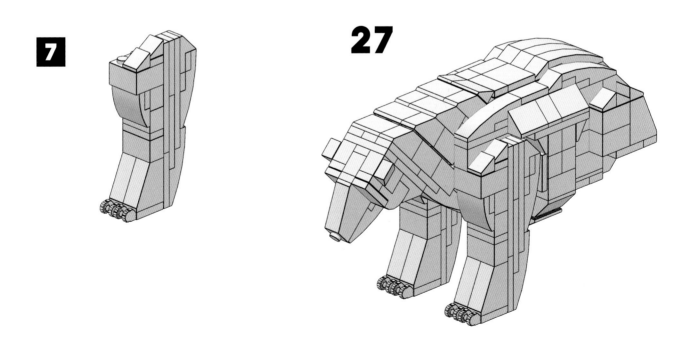

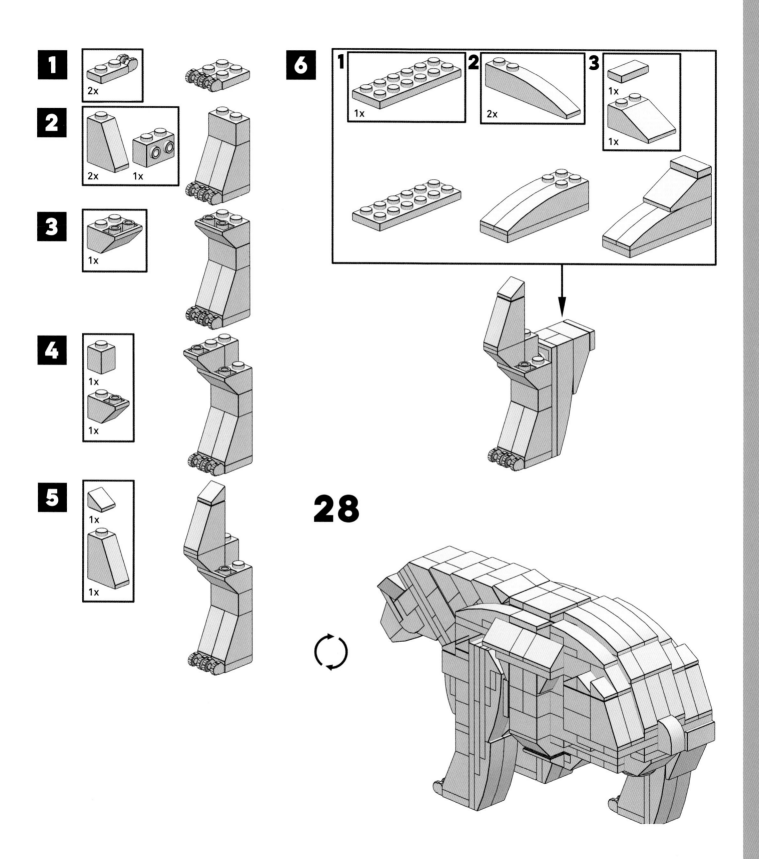

1 2x

2 2x 1x

3 1x

4 1x 1x

5 1x 1x

6 **1** 1x **2** 2x **3** 1x 1x

28

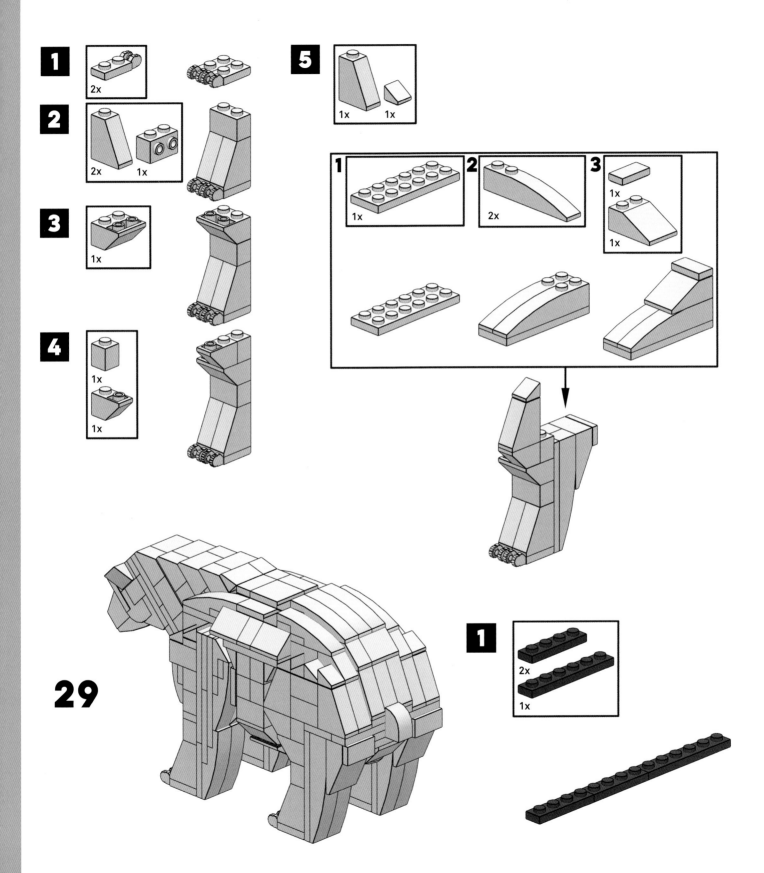

1 2x

2 2x 1x

3 1x

4 1x 1x

5 1x 1x

1 1x **2** 2x **3** 1x 1x

29

1 2x 1x

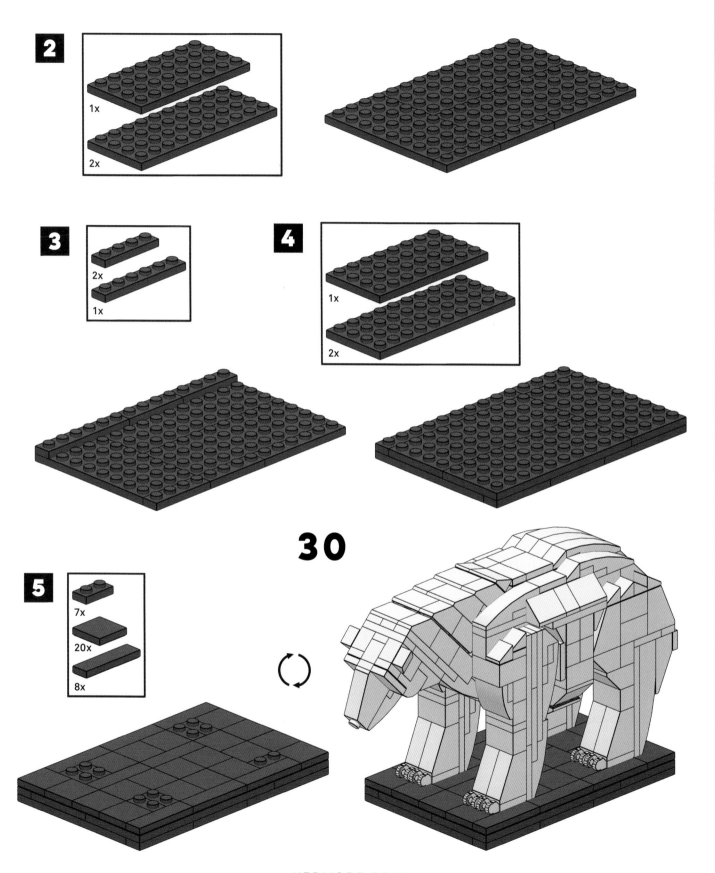

2

1x

2x

3

2x

1x

4

1x

2x

30

5

7x

20x

8x

GIANT ANTEATER

Myrmecophaga tridactyla

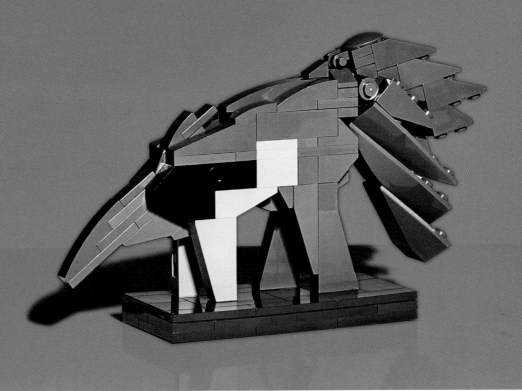

The giant anteater has one of the most interesting shapes of any animal I've ever seen, so I felt it was absolutely necessary that I challenge myself to build one. I really enjoy the geometric aesthetic of this sculpture, and the parts I used to capture the bushiness of its tail.

- The difference in size between anteater species is significant; the silky anteater is the size of a rodent, while the giant anteater is as long as a motorcycle.

- Anteaters do not keep each other company and prefer the solo lifestyle, with females only producing one offspring every 12 months.

- Despite having no teeth, anteaters are prolific eaters. Giant anteaters typically consume tens of thousands of ants and termites each day.

- Anteaters can be fierce when sensing danger, and their 4-inch (10 cm) claws are sharp enough to cause significant damage to anyone, or anything, that threatens it.

Parts Color Key

■	Black
■	Dark bluish gray
■	Dark green
■	Light bluish gray

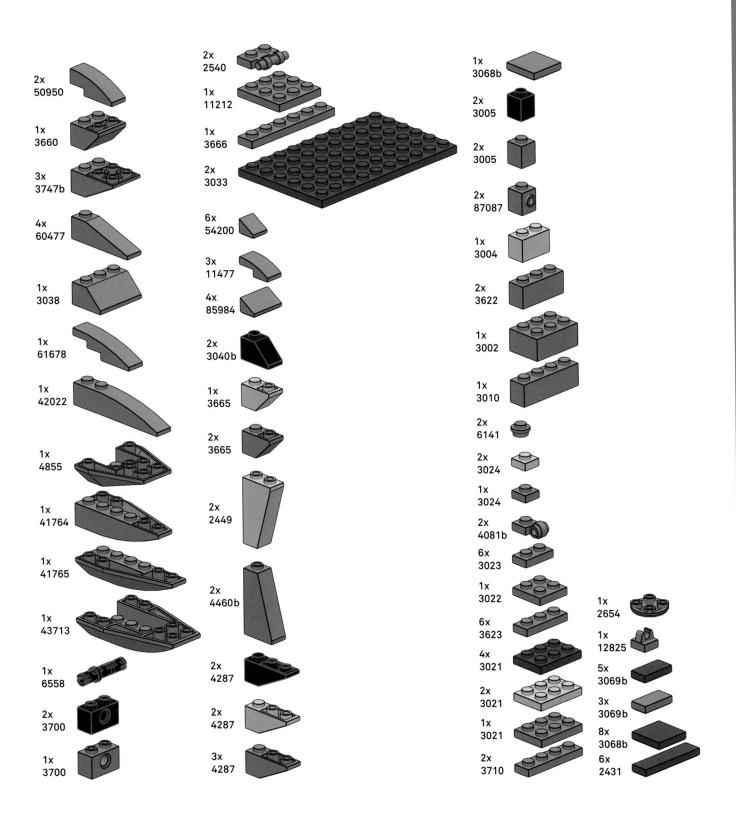

2x
50950

1x
3660

3x
3747b

4x
60477

1x
3038

1x
61678

1x
42022

1x
4855

1x
41764

1x
41765

1x
43713

1x
6558

2x
3700

1x
3700

2x
2540

1x
11212

1x
3666

2x
3033

6x
54200

3x
11477

4x
85984

2x
3040b

1x
3665

2x
3665

2x
2449

2x
4460b

2x
4287

2x
4287

3x
4287

1x
3068b

2x
3005

2x
3005

2x
87087

1x
3004

2x
3622

1x
3002

1x
3010

2x
6141

2x
3024

1x
3024

2x
4081b

6x
3023

1x
3022

6x
3623

4x
3021

2x
3021

1x
3021

2x
3710

1x
2654

1x
12825

5x
3069b

3x
3069b

8x
3068b

6x
2431

1

 1x
1x
3x

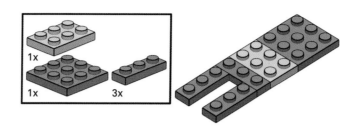

2

2x
1x
1x
1x

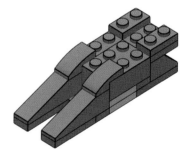

3

1x
1x
1x

4

2x
2x

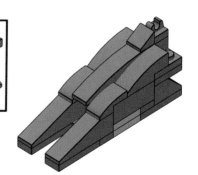

5

2x
1x

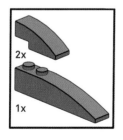

6

1x
1x

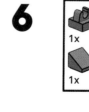

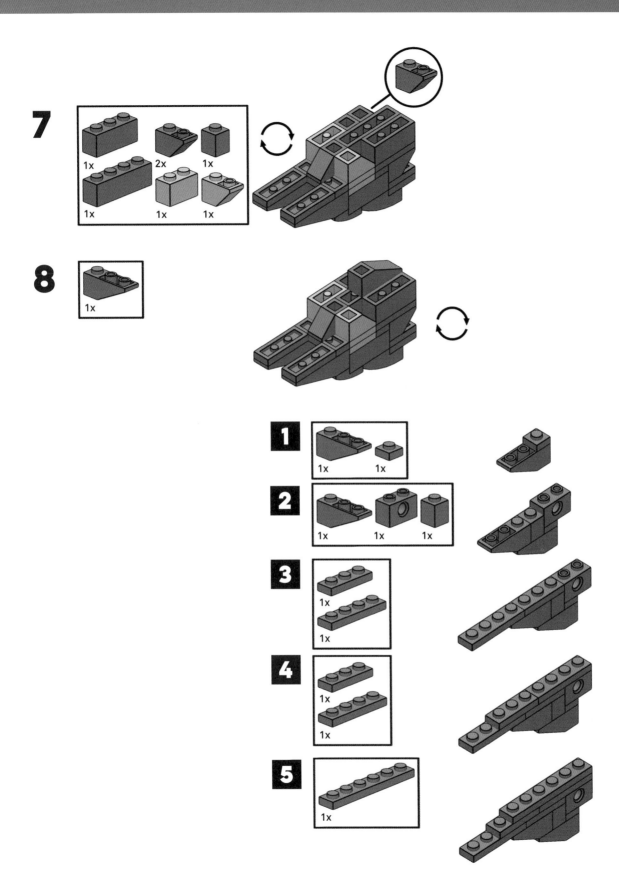

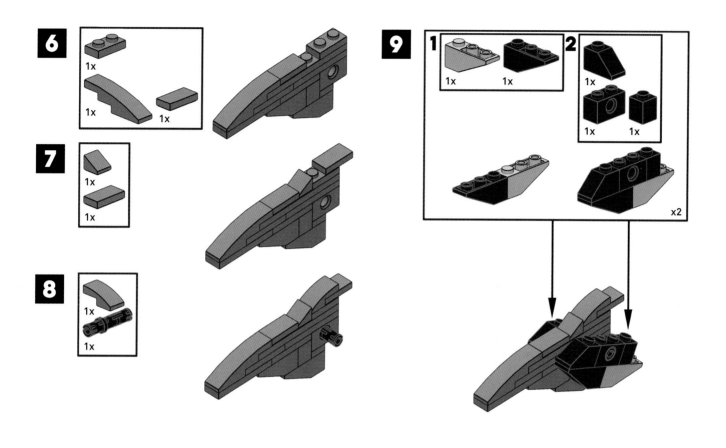

6
1x
1x 1x

7
1x
1x

8
1x
1x

9

1 1x 1x
2 1x 1x

x2

9

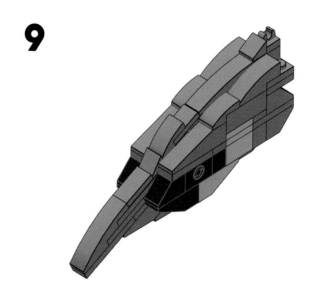

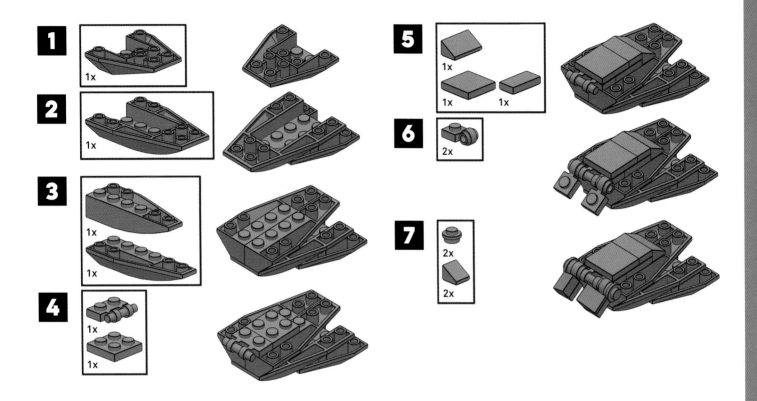

1 1x

2 1x

3 1x 1x

4 1x 1x

5 1x 1x 1x

6 2x

7 2x 2x

10

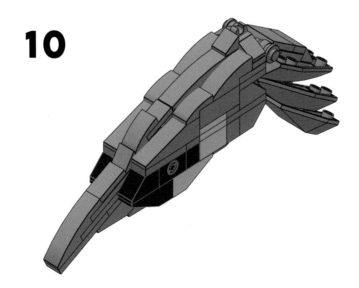

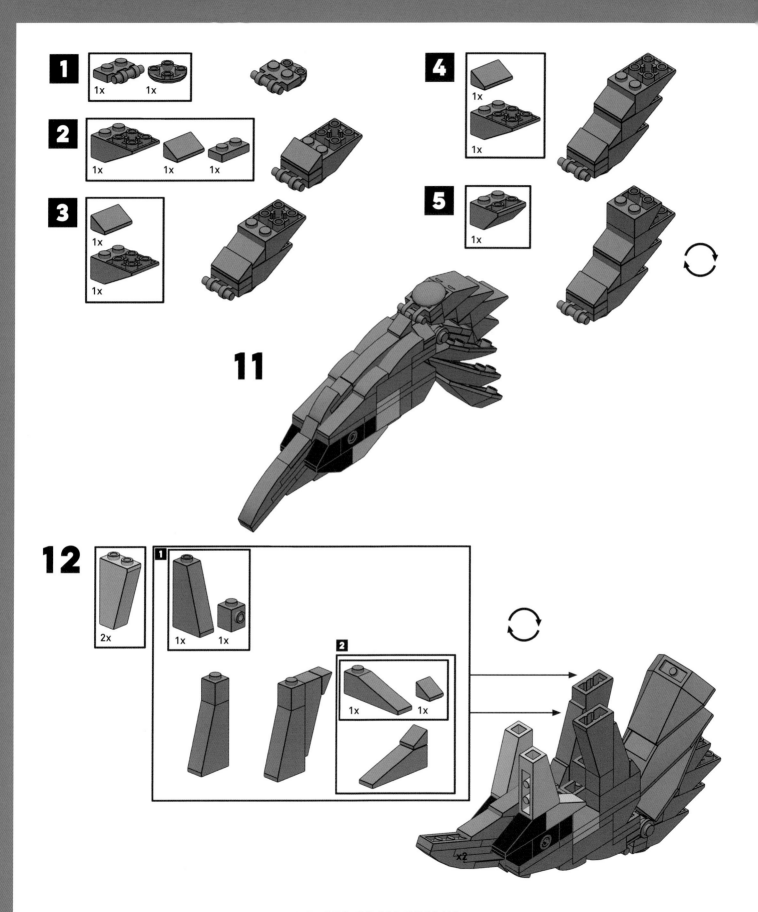

1 1x 1x

2 1x 1x 1x

3 1x 1x

4 1x 1x

5 1x

11

12 2x

1 1x 1x

2 1x 1x

x2

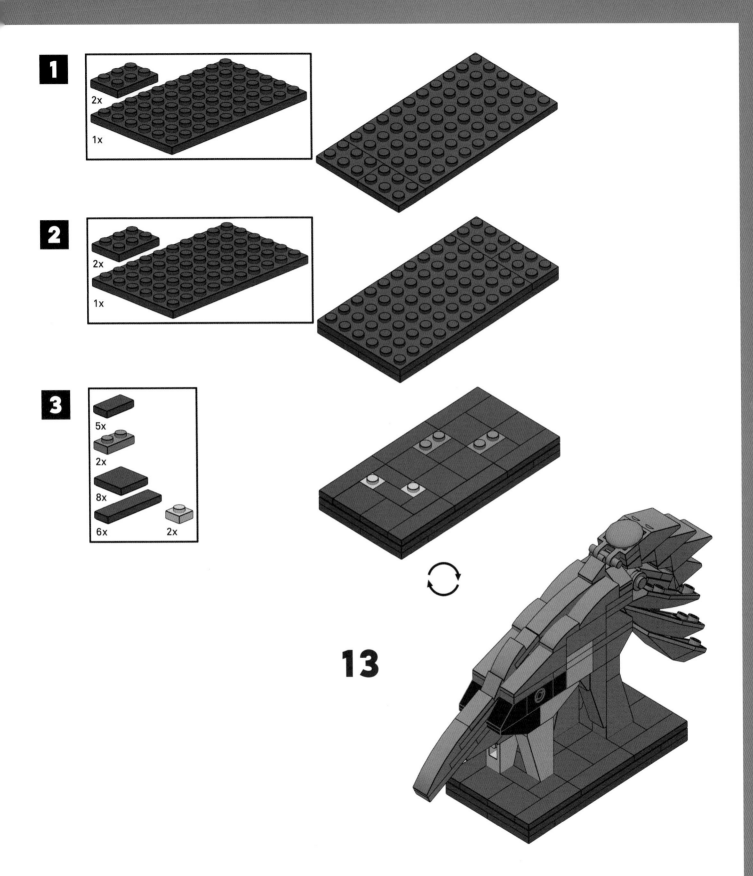

1
2x
1x

2
2x
1x

3
5x
2x
8x
6x   2x

13

PEALE'S DOLPHIN

Lagenorhynchus australis

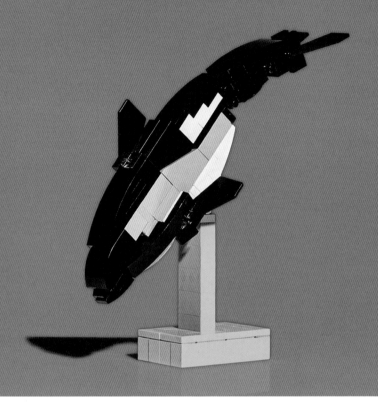

I always knew that I wanted to include a dolphin in this book, but I wasn't aware that there were so many species of them, particularly in the waters around South and Central America. In the end I chose Peale's dolphin due to its size, beautiful coloring, and documented acrobatic prowess.

- Like all dolphins, Peale's dolphins are highly social and can be found in groups of up to twenty, though much larger squads have been reported.

- Peale's dolphins typically enjoy a delightful diet of cephalopods, shellfish, and delectable bottom-feeders.

- Peale's dolphin was named after Titian Peale, who scholars maintain described the aquatic mammal in the 19th century.

Parts Color Key

- Black
- Light bluish gray
- Medium azure
- White

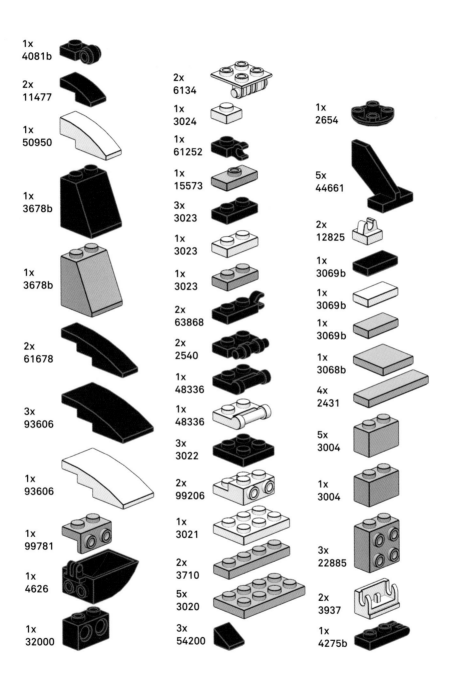

1x
4081b

2x
11477

1x
50950

1x
3678b

1x
3678b

2x
61678

3x
93606

1x
93606

1x
99781

1x
4626

1x
32000

2x
6134

1x
3024

1x
61252

1x
15573

3x
3023

1x
3023

1x
3023

2x
63868

2x
2540

1x
48336

1x
48336

3x
3022

2x
99206

1x
3021

2x
3710

5x
3020

3x
54200

1x
2654

5x
44661

2x
12825

1x
3069b

1x
3069b

1x
3069b

1x
3068b

4x
2431

5x
3004

1x
3004

3x
22885

2x
3937

1x
4275b

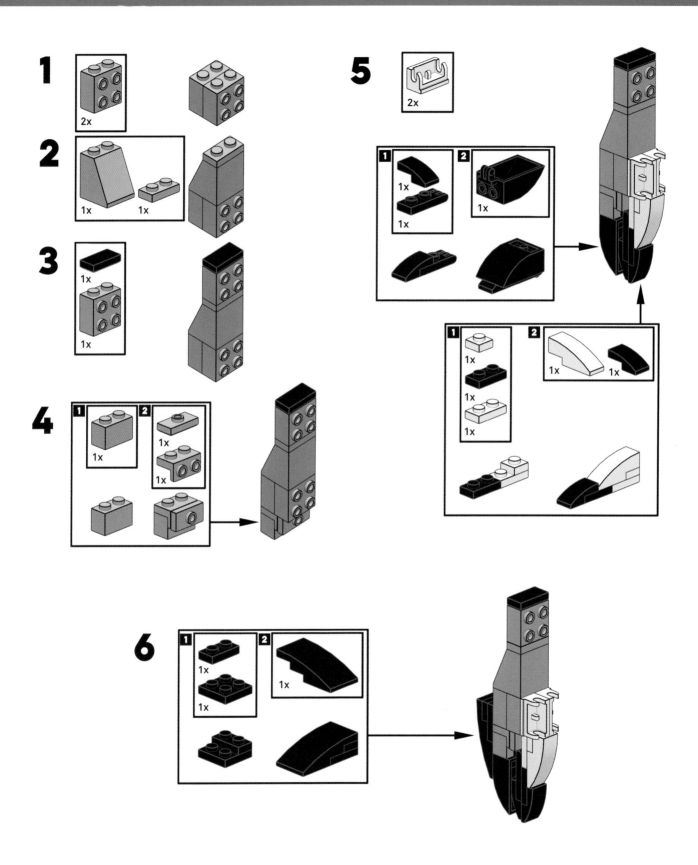

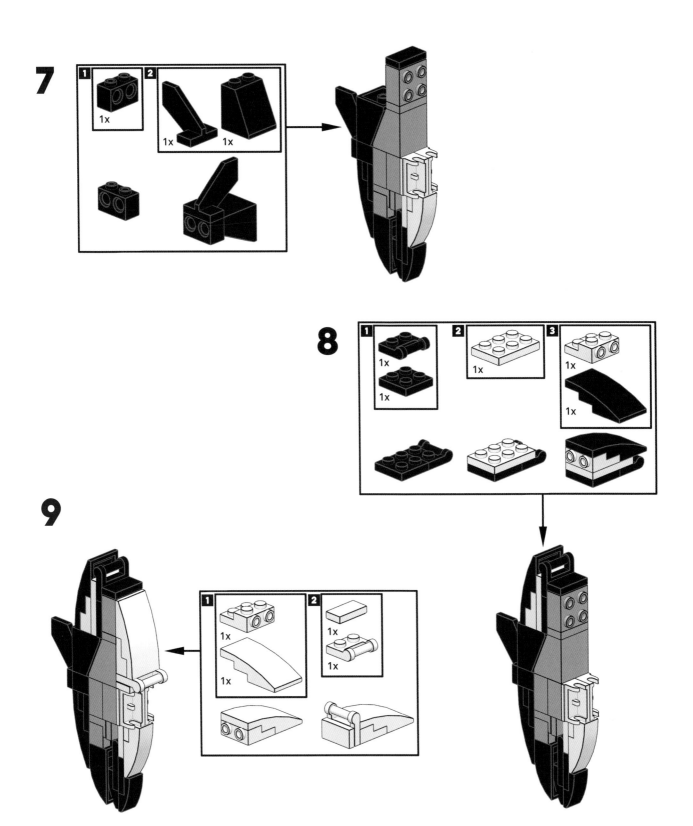

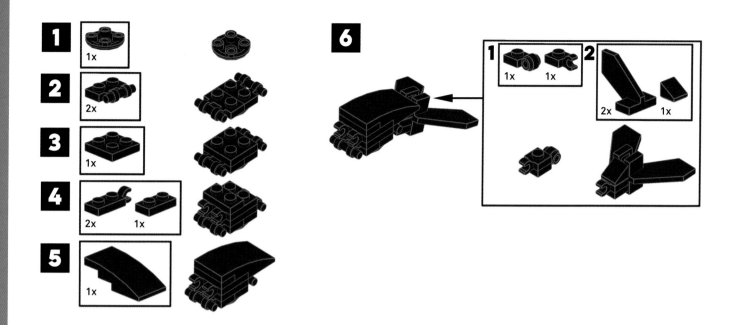

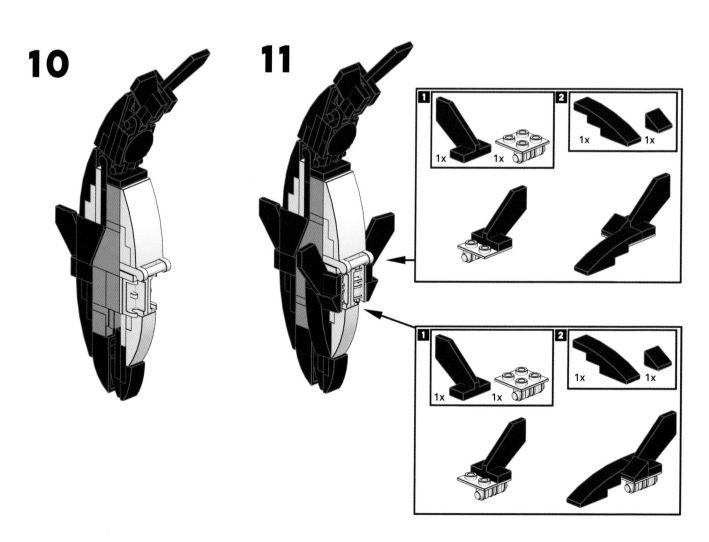

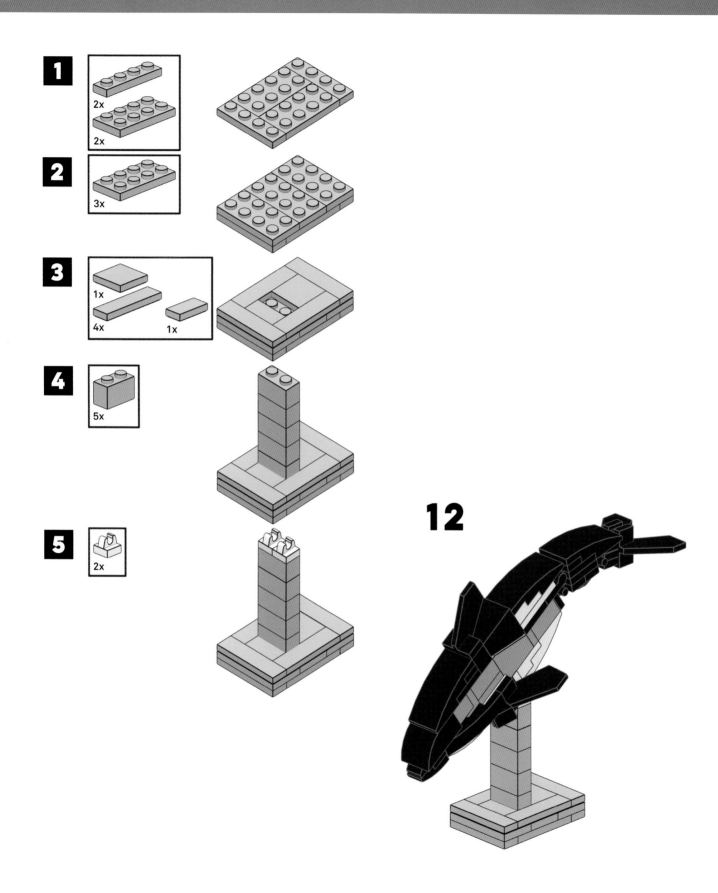

1 2x 2x

2 3x

3 1x 4x 1x

4 5x

5 2x

12

KOALA

Phascolarctos cinereus

Almost every photo I've seen of the eucalyptus-munching koala has it sitting snugly in a tree, so it only made sense for me to build one doing the same. The plinth for this sculpture is unique from the rest, too, in that it most closely resembles the form of the animal's natural habitat.

- The koala's main source of food is the poisonous eucalyptus leaf, which their unique digestive track is able to consume without any harmful effects.

- Koalas can climb trees with ease due to their sharp claws and opposable thumbs, and once up high, they rarely come down.

- With Australia's woodlands diminishing every year, the koala is in danger of losing its primary habitat.

Parts Color Key

- Black
- Dark bluish gray
- Reddish brown
- White

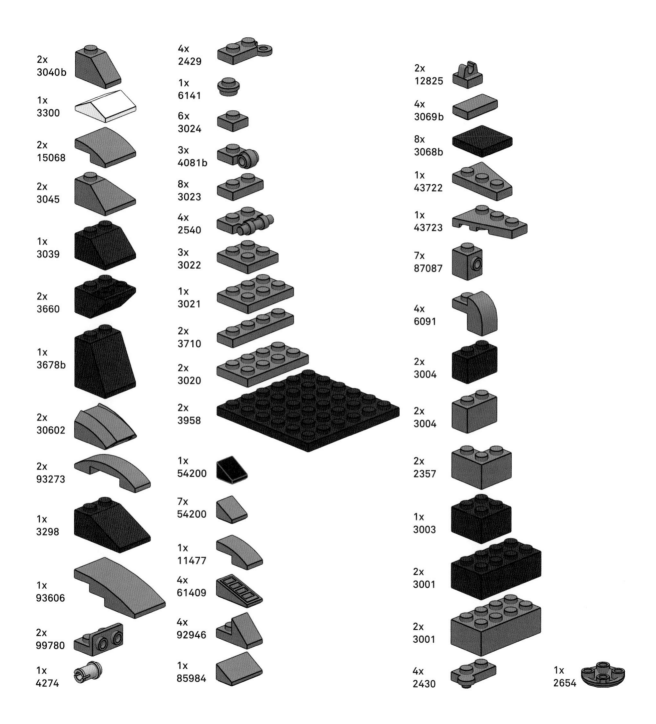

2x 3040b

1x 3300

2x 15068

2x 3045

1x 3039

2x 3660

1x 3678b

2x 30602

2x 93273

1x 3298

1x 93606

2x 99780

1x 4274

4x 2429

1x 6141

6x 3024

3x 4081b

8x 3023

4x 2540

3x 3022

1x 3021

2x 3710

2x 3020

2x 3958

1x 54200

7x 54200

1x 11477

4x 61409

4x 92946

1x 85984

2x 12825

4x 3069b

8x 3068b

1x 43722

1x 43723

7x 87087

4x 6091

2x 3004

2x 3004

2x 2357

1x 3003

2x 3001

2x 3001

4x 2430

1x 2654

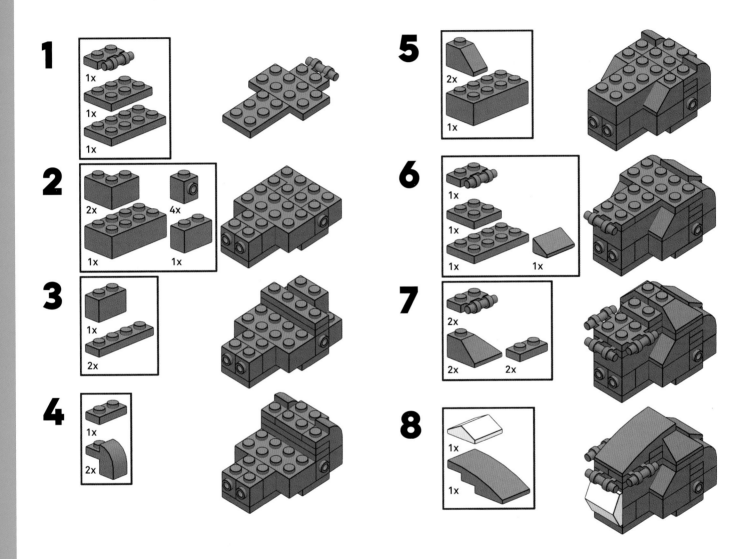

1

1x

1x

1x

2

2x

4x

1x

1x

3

1x

2x

4

1x

2x

5

2x

1x

6

1x

1x

1x

1x

7

2x

2x

2x

8

1x

1x

9

1x

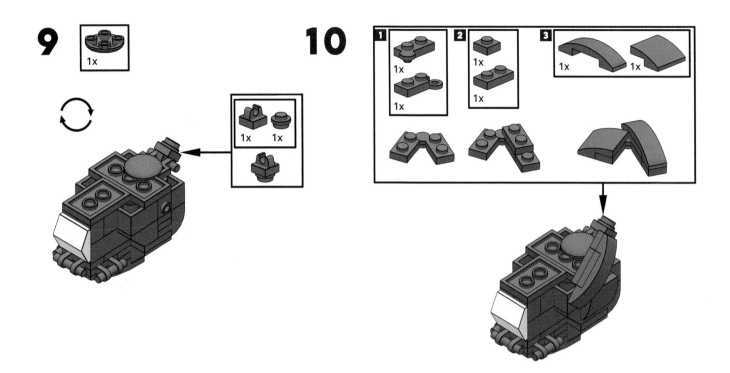

10

11

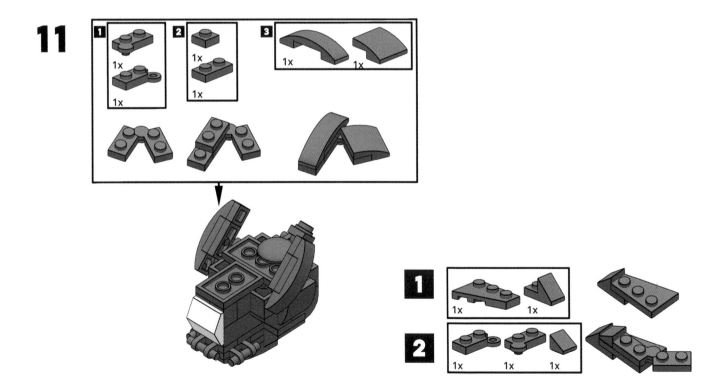

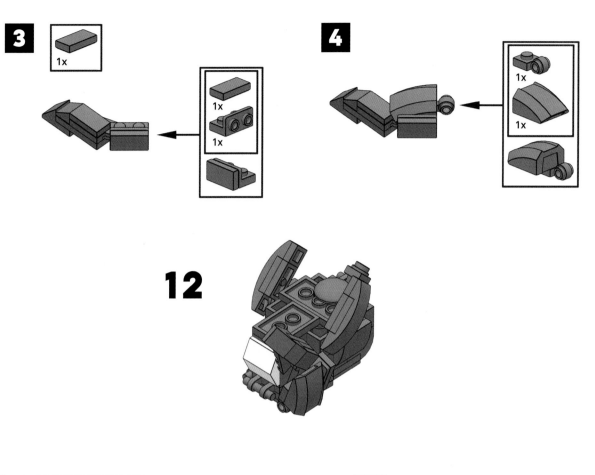

12

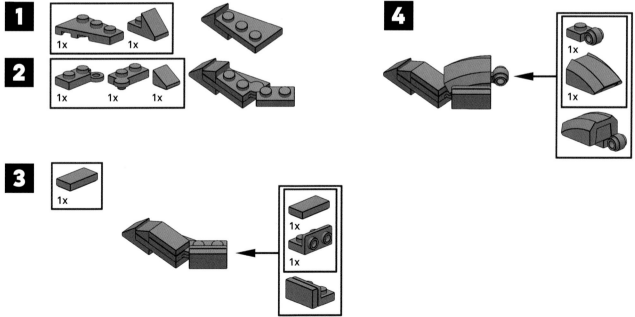

13

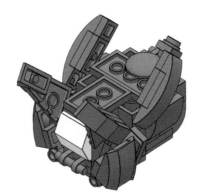

1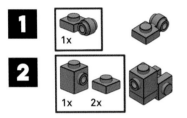
1x

2
1x 2x

3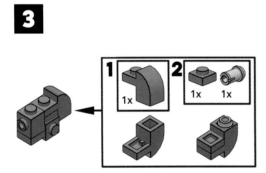
1 1x **2** 1x 1x

4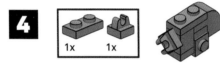
1x 1x

5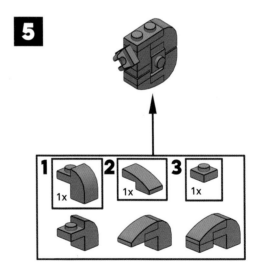
1 1x **2** 1x **3** 1x

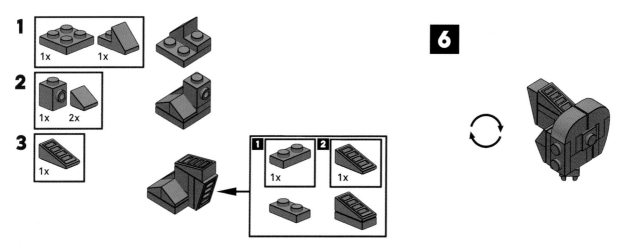

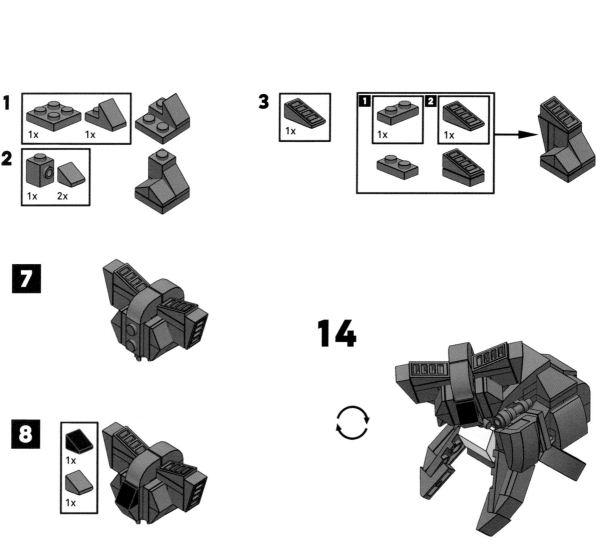

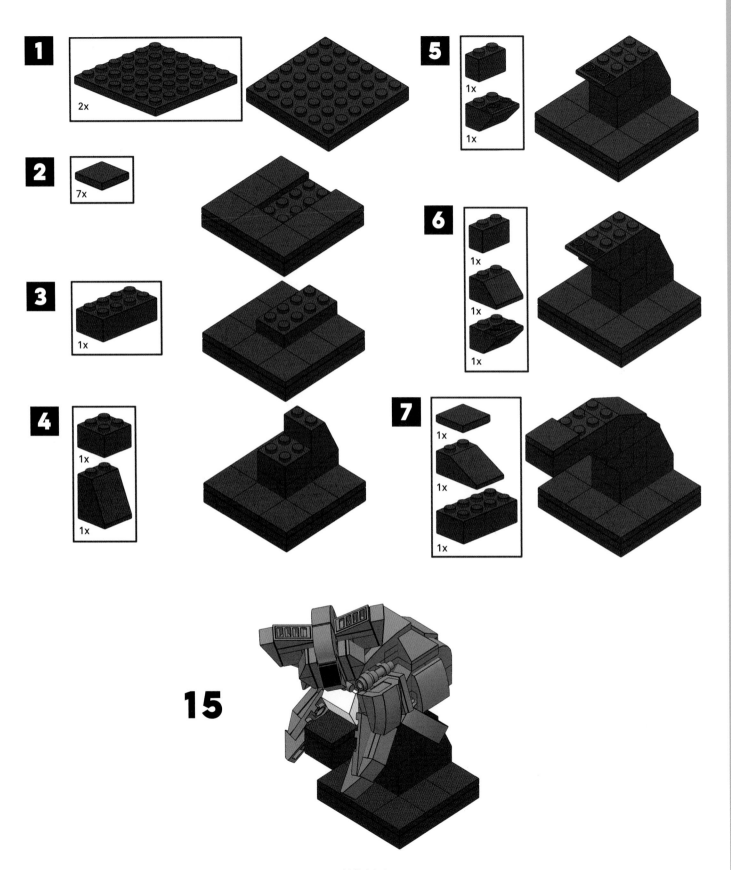

15

BARE-NOSED WOMBAT

common wombat

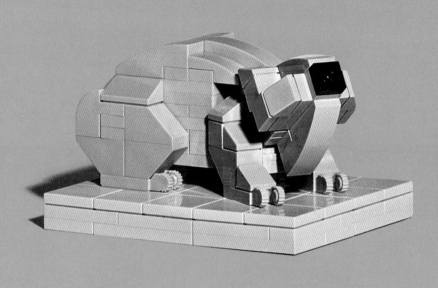

Found mainly in Australia, the bare-nosed wombat may look cute and cuddly, but it is often regarded as a pesky bandit for the vast networks of tunnels they burrow beneath agricultural fields and pastures. Despite its local infamy, I decided to build one for the people who, like myself, find roguery in a marsupial quite the charming attribute.

- As marsupials go, a wombat baby spends a lot of time in its mother's pouch after being born—up to 150 days before even taking its first step.

- Some wombat species live alone, but others live in large underground groups called colonies.

- Wombats are active at night, cutting through vegetation and tree bark with their sharp and ever-growing front incisors.

- Not all wombat species are endangered; those that aren't are typically hunted for sport or treated as a nuisance.

Parts Color Key

- ■ Black
- ▨ Light bluish gray
- ▨ Tan

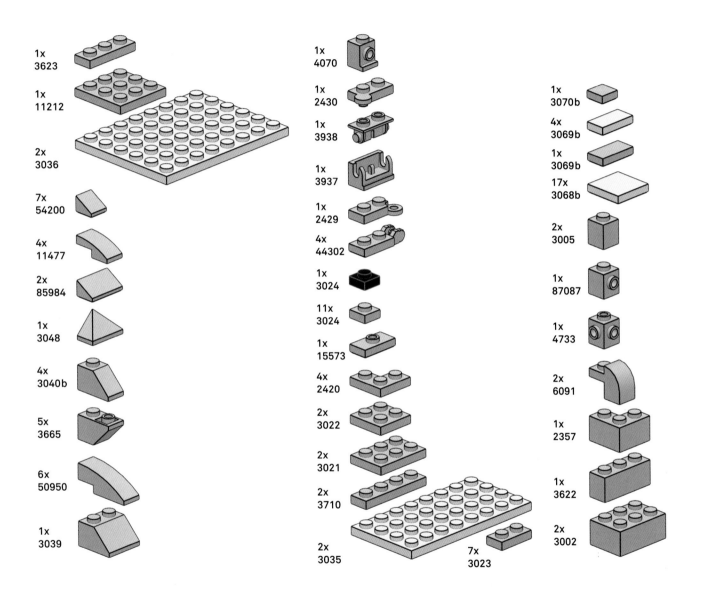

1x
3623

1x
11212

2x
3036

7x
54200

4x
11477

2x
85984

1x
3048

4x
3040b

5x
3665

6x
50950

1x
3039

1x
4070

1x
2430

1x
3938

1x
3937

1x
2429

4x
44302

1x
3024

11x
3024

1x
15573

4x
2420

2x
3022

2x
3021

2x
3710

2x
3035

7x
3023

1x
3070b

4x
3069b

1x
3069b

17x
3068b

2x
3005

1x
87087

1x
4733

2x
6091

1x
2357

1x
3622

2x
3002

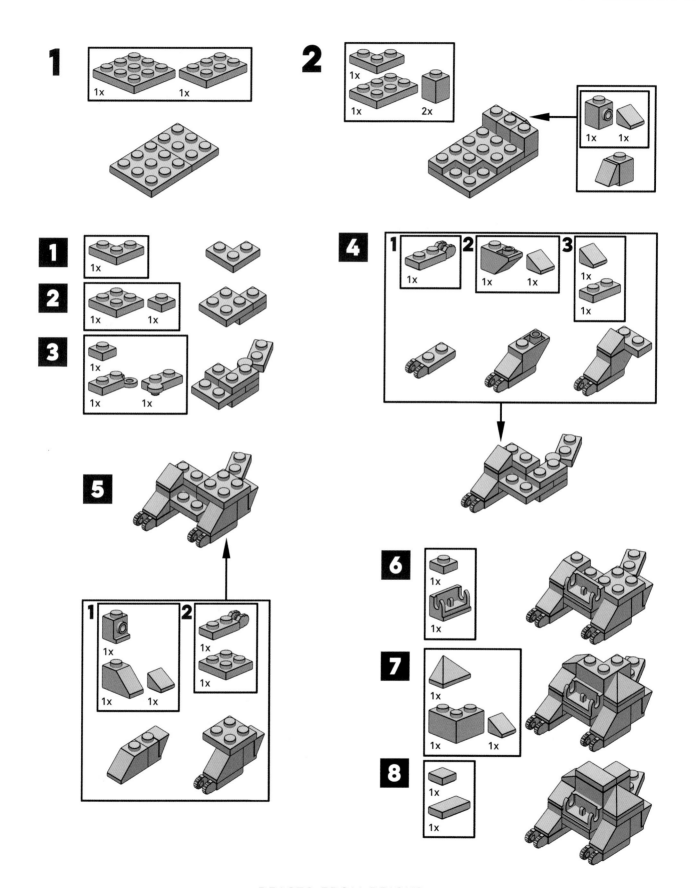

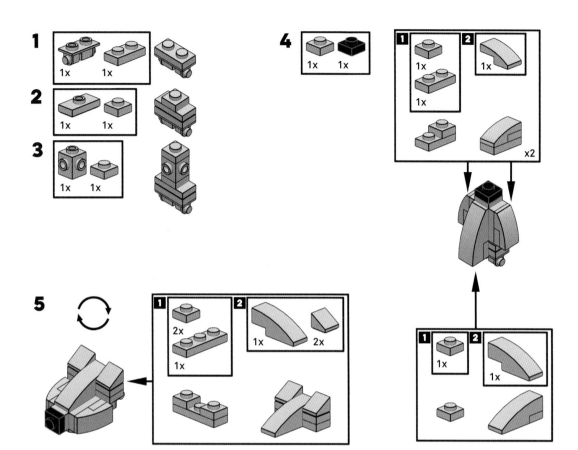

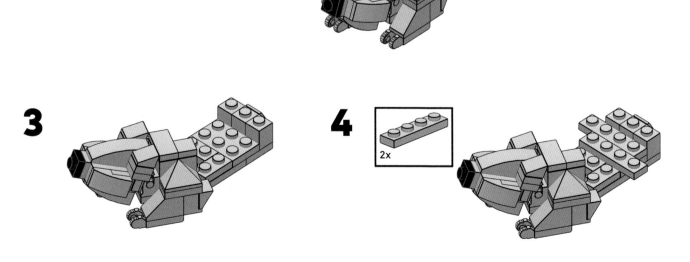

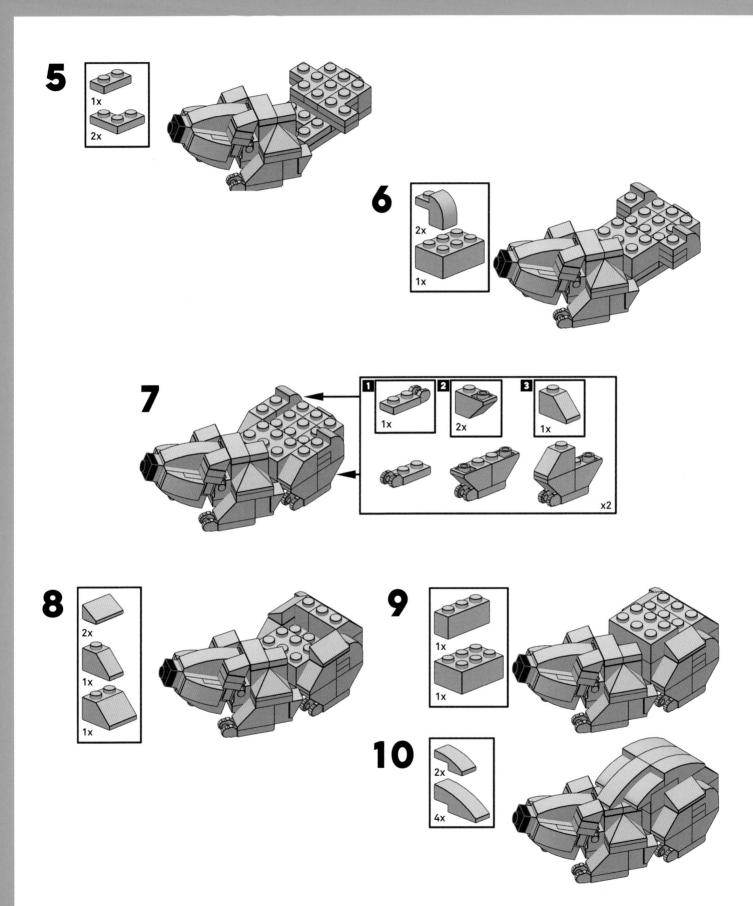

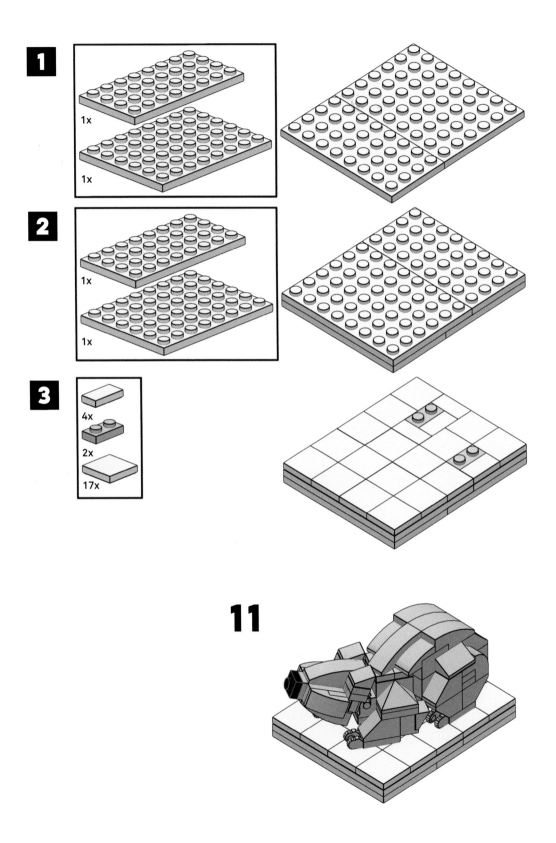

GALLERY

In this section, I share some of my more monumental and complex LEGO sculptures.

To give you a sense of scale, while *Winged Horse* and *Winged Unicorn* (opposite) were made with just 315 to 330 pieces, *Barn Owl* and *October Owl* (below) each required more than 2,000; the largest by far, *Silent Knight* (page 142), required 50,000.

BARN OWL
19" x 12" x 16"
(48.3 x 30.5 x 40.6 cm)
2,100 LEGO® elements

OCTOBER OWL
17" x 7.5" 17" (43.2 x 19 x 43.2 cm)
2,200 LEGO® elements

WINGED UNICORN
7½" x 7" x 7"
(19 x 17.8 17.8 cm)
330 LEGO®
elements

WINGED HORSE
7½" x 5" x 10"
(19 x 12.7 x 25.4 cm)
315 LEGO®
elements

SILENT KNIGHT
160" x 60" x 76"
(4 x 1.5 x 1.9 m)
50,000 LEGO®
elements

RESOURCES

Beasts

African Wildlife Foundation
www.awf.org

Arkive
www.arkive.org

Canadian Geographic
www.canadiangeographic.com

Encyclopedia Britannica
www.britannica.com

Encyclopedia of Life
www.eol.org

Knowledge Base Lookseek
knowledgebase.lookseek.com

National Geographic
www.nationalgeographic.com/animals

OneKind
www.onekind.org

Whale and Dolphin Conservation
www.whales.org

World Wildlife Federation
www.worldwildlife.org

Bricks

BrickLink
www.bricklink.com

Brickmania
www.brickmania.com

Brick Owl
www.brickowl.com

Bricks & Minifigs
www.bricksandminifigs.com

Brickset
www.brickset.com

Brickworld.com
www.brickworld.com

LEGO
www.lego.com

Swooshable
www.swooshable.com

The Brothers Brick
www.brother-brick.com

ABOUT THE AUTHOR

EKOW NIMAKO was born in Montreal and studied fine arts at York University. He began using LEGO® in his professional practice in 2013 and has since cultivated a unique approach to sculpting with the iconic material. In 2015, he explored the theme of animal extinction with his monumental sculpture *Silent Knight*, commissioned by the city of Toronto for Scotiabank Nuit Blanche. The seven-and-a-half-foot (2.3 m) sculpture paid homage to one of Ontario's most extirpated bird species, the barn owl, and was featured on CBC, *The Toronto Star*, and the Global Television Network. His 2016 public artwork *Grey Matters*, commissioned by the Baycrest Foundation for the citywide fundraising campaign *The Brain Project*, featured a monochromatic, larger-than-life human brain as a public statement about brain functionality and health. Ekow's current body of work, the progression of his 2014 exhibition *Building Black*, explores black identity through an Afro-surrealist lens, and will be exhibited in early 2018. Ekow lives and works in Toronto, Canada.